Doubling the Duality

Doubling the Duality: A Theoretical and Practical Investigation into Materiality and Embodiment of Meaning in the Integration of Live Action and Animation

By

Fabia Ling-Yuan Lin

CAMBRIDGE SCHOLARS

PUBLISHING

Doubling the Duality:
A Theoretical and Practical Investigation into Materiality and Embodiment of Meaning in the Integration of Live Action and Animation,
by Fabia Ling-Yuan Lin

This book first published 2014

Cambridge Scholars Publishing

12 Back Chapman Street, Newcastle upon Tyne, NE6 2XX, UK

British Library Cataloguing in Publication Data
A catalogue record for this book is available from the British Library

ISBN (10): 1-4438-5550-2, ISBN (13): 978-1-4438-5550-1

to farm animals

TABLE OF CONTENTS

LIST OF FILM PRACTICES

Nothing to Do with Weather	**2009**
Stop-frame, hand-drawn, 3-D computer animation; digital compositing.	3’50”
Animating Animator the Animated	**2011**
Pixilation, hand-drawn animation; live action; digital compositing.	8’27”
Flying Tunes	**2012**
Pixilation, 3-D computer animation; live action; digital compositing.	2’47”

PREFACE

This book is based on my PhD thesis for Loughborough University, the outcome of a practice-led research undertaken from 2007 to 2013. The original thesis is comprised of a body of work (hybrid films) and its contextual analysis. Being both the source and product of the themes expressed in the written thesis, the practical component of the project consists of three hybrid films: *Nothing to Do with Weather* (3'50"), *Animating Animator the Animated* (2'47"), and *Flying Tunes* (8'27"). Since all the films can be accessed online, they are not attached with this book.

Aiming at understanding and re-interpreting the dialogical relationship between live action and animation, this research argues that from its beginning the art of moving images has presented a struggle between opposed tendencies – such as "imprint" and "construction", "machine eye" and "artist's hand", "dissection of time" and "condensation of time"– that are found between the unstable duality of live action and animation. While mainstream cinema has focused most of its efforts on taming the collisions that occur within the integration of live action and animation, it has also relied on the interface's instability to animate its being. As the interface becomes more invisible in the digital age, this research reconsiders the interaction between live action and animation in moving-image production and the construction of meaning in filmmaking as it incorporates the digital into its languages.

Before the PhD study, I worked in a multimedia company as an animation designer in Taiwan. But my media career actually started from making documentary films at a TV station. My animated works, therefore, often presented the meeting between aspects of animation and live action in some way. The consistent interest in the possibility of the integration of live action and animation became the subject matter of the PhD study. However, the whole PhD journey was not just about tensions between the two media, it was also about the collision between creative practice and systematic inquiry. And most of all, it was about the encounter between different cultures.

Because of a desire to know what the highest academic degree for animation would be like, I left the comforts of life I was having then, flying halfway round the world, to join the practice-led research programme at Loughborough University. As it was quite common among international students who had to stay for an extended period to complete the study, I experienced profound culture shock. I went through the loneliness and sterile bitterness of a person who was abruptly isolated from her established network; but I also came across the sweetest friendship and the most passionate and creative moments in my life. All the anxiety, distress and illness were mixed with excitement, exoticism and a dreamy quality. It turned out to be an exceptionally memorable adventure, and a weirdly productive time. Overall it seemed to demonstrate a well-known saying: "the days you are most uncomfortable are the days you learn most about yourself", and understanding is the foundation for meaningful change to happen. This, as far as I am concerned, applies to the encounter between live action and animation as well.

I owe much to the various kinds of encouragement, support and commentary that have come from friends and colleagues during those years. Yun-Ju Chen and Ching-Chun Huang have been highly supportive even when we were on opposite sides of the earth; they also offered direct help in my practical endeavour.

For their constant encouragement and close support I would particularly like to single out Lingqi Kong, Xinyi Wang, James Lee and Anna Yang. Chunyan Wu has made the final stage of the study far more colourful than days waiting for examination and submission could be. I owe an especial debt to Harry Gui, a fascinating hybrid of Chinese and British cultures who I was very lucky to know from my first year in the UK. He has been a vital friend, landlord and intellectual prompter who pulled me through the study with humor and discerning critical suggestions.

For the support I received in completing the degree I should like to thank my supervisors Johanna Hällsten and Paul Wells. I am particularly grateful to Marion Arnold, Director of Research Rrogrammes at School of the Arts, for her invaluable comments upon the thesis and help of many kinds. I would never have finished the thesis had I not met Jayne Pilling in the final stage. She read the whole manuscript and offered the most crucial help with the revision when it was most needed. It is with great affection and gratitude that I mention her here.

My parents and siblings have never questioned my choice of career pursuit. Their unreserved support has allowed me to gain achievement from my acts of daring and wondering. I would also like to thank my partner, Wei-Chien Wu, whose relentless encouragement gave me confidence whenever I was subdued by self-doubt. Throughout the six-year leaving his faith and patience continually gave me strength to take various kinds of challenges.

INTRODUCTION

0.1 Background and Aims of Research

The primary aim of this thesis is to contribute to the field of animated filmmaking through a consideration of its theoretical framework and the submission of a body of work (three hybrid films). The contextualisation of the films re-interprets the relationship between live action and animation for filmmaking. The second aim is to raise the awareness of the interface between live action and animation in moving-image production through the discovery and construction of meaning in filmmaking as it incorporates the digital into its languages.

Live action and animation have a dialogical relationship that dates back to the beginning of the invention of the cinematic device. There have been discussions about their different natures, roles and functions and about how their qualities oppose or supplement each other. For example, while most independent animated films are characterised by a high degree of physical and aesthetic intervention and engagement from the artist, live-action film is usually described as a product of machine vision that informs the realistic aesthetic traditions of cinema (Benjamin 1992 [1935]: 213; Kracauer 1960: 28; Manovich 2001:307) (this will be discussed in Chapter 1). The relationship between live action and animation appears to speak for the opposed tendencies embraced across the field of moving image. However, the advent of digital technologies has brought about changes in their relationship.

Digital technologies are so powerful that animated images can easily be mixed with live action without this being recognised. As a result, as Manovich points out (2001: 295), "cinema can no longer be clearly distinguished from animation". Moreover, the reintroduction of manual processes and the privileged role they can play in digital cinema may have turned cinema into a particular category of painting, making the "kino-eye" become a "kino-brush" (Monovich (2001: 308). Overall the digital seems to promise two things: the first relates to freedom of expression, and the second to the renaissance of animation. For the first, digital technologies have the capacity to realise the filmmakers' desire to be freed from live action film's indexical nature and its inclination to realism. The availability of affordable and technologically advanced personal computers also makes it possible for filmmakers to get rid of traditional equipment, which is expensive and bulky, and thus to escape the complex organisational structure of big studios. As for the second issue, the newer methods of computer-based postproduction represent a return of pre-cinematic moving-image techniques such as hand-painting and hand-animating; this can make filmmaking a subset of animation so as to redeem animation's role in cinema.

It has now been more than twenty years since the release of Adobe Premiere, the first popular digital video editing application. The production of moving images in mainstream cinema, however, does not present the riotous profusion that could be realised through the availability and capacity of digital imaging technology. On the contrary, it appears to converge around an even more homogenous aesthetic. The dominant aesthetic seems not so different from that of the pre-digital era. For example, digital tools are powerful and convenient tools with which to create different kinds of integration of heterogeneous elements; yet instead of making the interface between live action and animation more varied and intriguing, the accommodation of digital tools seems to have merely enhanced the hegemony of a few dominant aesthetics such as photorealism and seamless compositing (which will be discussed in detail in Chapter 1).

The performance of "photographicness" (North 2008: 12) as a principle illusory strategy in digital cinema also undermines the idea of animation's revival (in Manovich et al's sense) because what digital tools facilitate may not be what some (classical or experimental) animators might consider to be animation. Mainstream cinema's pursuit of photorealism seems to efface and repress computer-generated imagery's potential to be a subversive and liberated form of animation. Thus, as North (2008: 12) argues: "perhaps animation is merely pretending to be part of mainstream cinema, sneaking back in to acceptance by disguising itself as photography, following its banishment to the realms of children's entertainment in the early decades of the twentieth century".

Under these circumstances, I felt an urge to re-examine and recognise the relationship between live action and animation, to explore the vitality of the interface between them, and the function of digital technologies in terms of their integration. As a film practitioner from eastern Asia, I was trained and received most of my creative experience in Taiwan, and I consider that the cultural identity of the researcher is inevitably reflected in his/her practice and thesis. My research is, therefore, responsive not only to the events of digitalisation but also to some extent to the issues of my own experiences of different cultures, and different traditions of image making.

The title of the thesis uses the term "doubling the duality" to indicate my views of the relationship between live action and animation as a permeable interplay between emergent and receding aspects inherent in their integration. This standpoint, I believe, is worth exploring not only by theorists but also by practitioners. Scholars such as Darley (2000), Manovich (2001) and McClean (2008) have discussed the relationship between live action and animation at length, but in those discussions the relationship is not seen as unstable or to possess playful dualities, which is, in part, the focus of this study. In some academic texts, e.g. Broadfoot & Bulter (1991), Cholodenko (1991b), Clancy (1991) and Riggs (2007), the relationship is examined from deconstructionist standpoints and described as dynamic and mobile. However these are mainly voices from theorists that are not derived from the making of practice. On the premise that understandings derived from practice are also crucial for knowledge, this study hopes to enrich the discussions about the relationship from my double role as both a practitioner and a theorist. Moreover, although carried out in the UK within Western academic paradigms, I hope my being a non-Westerner and having the experience of filmmaking within Taiwanese culture can bring a cross-cultural dimension to the research that will further enhance and contribute to the diversity of existing discussions.

The notion of "doubling the duality" reflects some basic concerns of this study, including the nature of the cinematic apparatus, an inclination to question hierarchies and distinctions in the digital age, and my idea of what constitutes an artistic practice. "Doubling the duality" does not simply indicate a repetitive use of the dialectic or a balanced pairing; rather, the notion can be discussed with reference to a number of philosophical concepts, especially those having benefited thinkers in the film and animation disciplines.

The Deconstruction of Presence

Deconstruction is a poststructuralist theory introduced by the French philosopher Jacques Derrida. He first employs the term "deconstruction" in *Of Grammatology* (1967). One of its key assumptions is the undermining of binary opposition. For Derrida, the structures of binary opposition that are essential to logocentric language are actually hierarchies, defined not simply by differences but by the privileging of one term at the expense of the other (Derrida 1981: 42-44). Deconstruction contends that such hierarchies can be inverted, and the opposition can be undermined or collapsed. Furthermore, everything is comprised of opposed tendencies and is in a state of becoming rather than a fixed, static being.

Deleuze and Guattari (1987: 238) stress that becomings are not evolutionary but symbiotic, resulting in alliances between disparate entities which, in themselves, are actually unimportant to the principle of becoming and they note, "What is real is the becoming itself, the block of becoming, not the supposedly fixed terms through which that which becomes passes". In this sense, when we say something is animation, this is actually pointing out its state of "becoming-animation", and likewise live action means a state of "becoming-live action". They themselves are in a continuous and mobile state. The integration of animation and live action therefore is a doubling of duality, where "dual" becomes "ambidual" (meaning "both-are-double"; see Fordham 2007: iii), and the hybrid figure on the screen becomes a becoming of two becomings. The opposed attributes between live action and animation are interdependent, and their integration, as I will suggest in Chapter 1, makes the hybridised figures playful riddles that have multiple meanings.

Potential for the Subversive

Although the distinctions between live action and animation are often flexible and mutable, exploring the seemingly opposed qualities between live action and animation is still useful in understanding moving images. Deleuze (2004: 32-33) considers that all identities are effects of difference. Not only are no two things ever the same, the categories we use to identify individuals in the first place derive from differences. Moreover, we cannot think about the notion of becoming without considering the difference. Deleuze and Guattari (1987: 245) emphasise the radical difference at the heart of becoming. For them, "such difference serves as a questioning of traditional methods of thinking which presuppose the unshakeable existence of truth and error." Therefore, the idea of seeing things as becomings reveals the construction of meanings, and also that of "values". Not surprisingly the integration of live action and animation, the becoming of becomings is often employed by artists in a reflexive way to express their political perspectives (for example, in Gehman & Reinke 2005 and Wells & Hardstaff 2008). A dynamic relation is initiated by "difference", as Deleuze uses this concept. While intending to mobilise cinematic imagery by recognising it as an unstable and undecidable becoming, I start the exploration by looking for incompatible meanings within it. By "teasing out the warring forces" (Johnson 1980: 5) of figuration within cinematic imagery, the integration of live action and animation – with a mutable, supplemented and ever-changing relationship between them – can serve both an aesthetic, and political purpose (in terms of challenging the status quo).

Connection with the Uncanny

The term "double" recalls that of the "doppelganger", one of the key aspects in Freud's notion of the "uncanny". He suggests in the 1919 essay "*Das Unheimlich*" that the feeling of the uncanny would be at its peak when it is triggered by the reappearance of a familiar object that has been forgotten or repressed for a long time (Freud 2009: 129). It has to do with the return of what is forgotten but has frightened us in our childhood or, anthropologically speaking, the childhood of the human (2009: 156-157). Moreover, the uncanny is bound to Freud's notion of the death drive. It is death that returns (149). Cholodenko (1991: 28) has an intriguing comment on the bond between the uncanny and the notion of the death drive illustrated by Freud:

> In *Beyond the Pleasure Principle* Freud speculates that the human comes from the inanimate and that there is a death drive which leads the human to his/her own proper death, the restoration to the inanimate state from which one came. Such a death drive keeps one alive to find one's proper death; and therefore, the death drive is indistinguishable from a life drive, or better, the death drive is both life and death drive at the same time. It suggests that life is never without its death at the same time, even that in a sense we have not one but two deaths – the one which precedes us, the one which awaits us – and a third as well – the one which lives with us.

What it implies would advance both notions of animation and of live action: animation always has something of the inanimate about it; likewise live action always embodies the corpse in itself. The inescapable antithesis within each of them both "allows" and "disallows" their being them. As a result, as an extension of Cholodenko's statement, in a sense the uncanny is always with us in the act of integrating live action and animation.

Research Questions

Grounding

This research is an inquiry into how to find ways to realise a sense of estrangement; yet in the earliest phases, the main part of this research was generated by the following preliminary questions:

1) In live-action/animated hybrid films, how could an animation filmmaker define and interrogate the relationship between live-action and animated elements?
2) How does contemporary digital image technology function in the relationship between live-action and animated elements in live-action/animated hybrid cinema?

These questions emerged from the animated film *Nothing to Do with Weather* (2009), developed during my first year of research. I wanted to create a piece of work that demonstrates as many examples of the interfaces between live action and animation as possible. In the actual process of making I tested, and experimented with, the combination of animated and live-action elements within the confrontation between character and environment, character and character, environment and environment. The process and results facilitated locating key aspects from my work that exploit the tension between live action and animation as some of its focus.

To offer a more detailed understanding of the preoccupations driving this research, a number of salient conceptual points in *Nothing to Do with Weather* are summarised below. There is no specific storyline. Most of the scenes come from my illustrated diary[1] made in the first year of my study abroad when the feeling of dislocation was intense and disturbing. The film begins with the sound of rain and a corner of a sitting room with an empty sofa (fig. 0-1a). The protagonist enters, takes a seat and draws a girl on the drawing pad. She gives her a cup of tea and a book (fig. 0-1b). The girl on the pad opens the book, sips the tea, and then starts a tour in the 2-dimensional hand-drawn world (fig. 0-1c, 0-1d, 0-1e, 0-1f). At the end of the tour she falls into the photographic world and settles on the sofa. After returning the cup to the photographic protagonist, she leaves the corner (fig. 0-1g). And we are back to the opening scene again (fig. 0-1h).

The sitting room scenes are made using stop-frame photography, which makes the photographic figure[2] a frame-by-frame manipulation. The conceptual points I identified in this practice emphasise questions around: (1) a dynamic duality; (2) the tension between live action and animation and the experience of estrangement; (3) the negation of the codes of realism.

---

[1] Part of the diary can be accessed online from my personal blog: http://blog.yam.com/fabia

[2] I use the term 'figure' when discussing characters in the film in order to stress its figuration, its image, its representation.

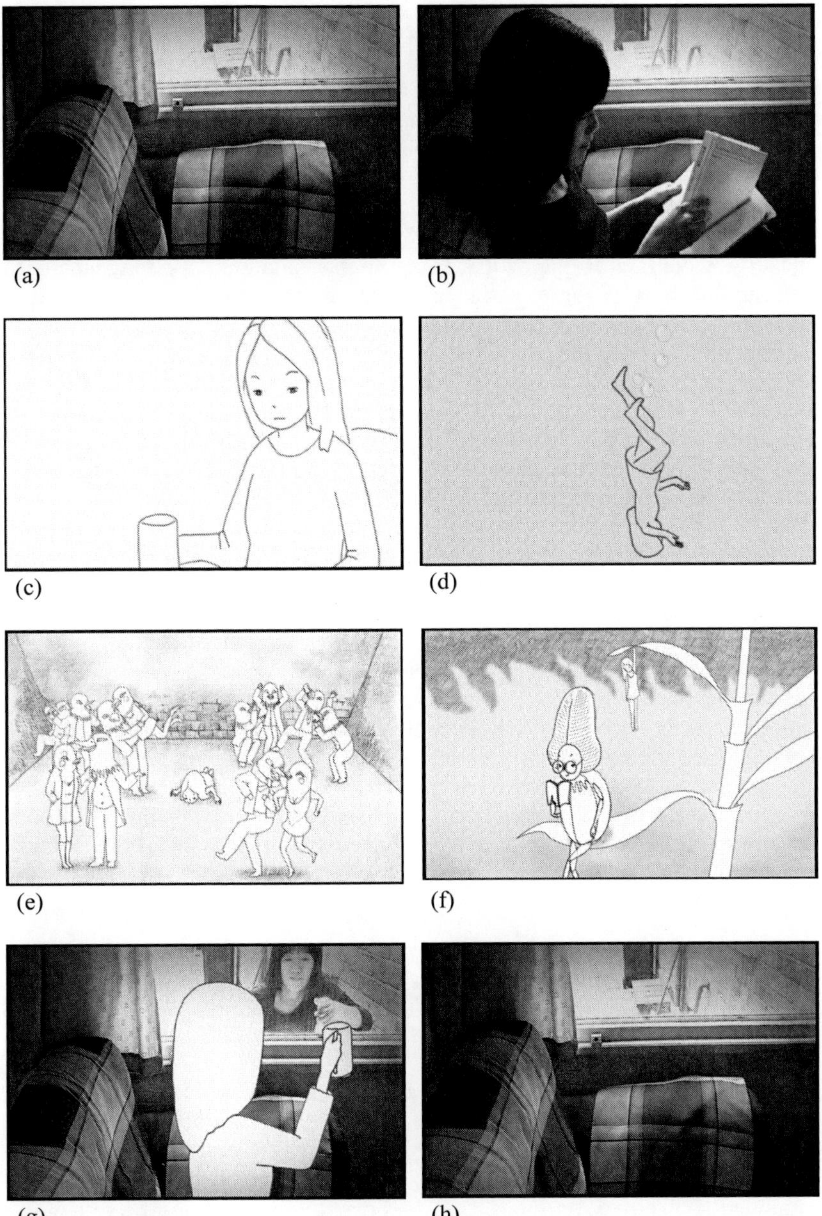

Fig. 0-1: Stills from Nothing to Do with Weather *(2009, 3'50")*

The first question is to explore live action's and animation's opposed attributes in the process of film-making, and the visual result of their integration or juxtaposition in different ways. The second relates to how experiential estrangement informs the manipulation of materiality. That fact that this practice is built on my illustrations, which reflect the inner experience of my first-year adventure of studying abroad, inevitably makes it an attempt to combine visual material with experiential issues. Moreover, the situation depicted in this practice reminded me of Freud's uncanny, which, as Royle (2003:2) comments, is about "a strangeness of framing and borders, an experience of liminality". This leads to a further investigation of aesthetic estrangement.

The third question explores negating or challenging established codes. There are two attempts to integrate different techniques within a character in this practice: the photographic figure made by frame-by-frame manipulation, and a hand-drawn figure traced from a 3-D computer generated model in some sequences. I noticed the intriguing effect of frame-by-frame photography (which soon developed into my experiments with pixilation throughout the project); I also noticed the hampered movement performed by the hand-drawn figure due to the combination of a 3-D computer model (with its rigging being very simple). A hypothesis therefore emerged: when the integration happens within the character, there may be conflict or inconsistency between the figuration of the body and its performance – for example, caricatured figures are expected to have cartoony performance, while characters making up and dressing up in a naturalistic way may be expected to perform in a more realistic manner – and this may become a source of aesthetic estrangement. This then led me to this project's core experiment: integrating photographic imagery and cartoon's hyperrealistic performance.

Through the cyclic research process described later in this introduction, the initial research questions were repeatedly clarified and refined, and became the main question described below.

Main Question

How can the integration of the opposing attributes between live action and animation interrupt perceptual realism and produce a sense of estrangement in a meaningful way?

In this research it is considered crucial to develop practice strategies that would link existential and aesthetic estrangement appropriately, and to reflect the condition of existence by expressing it both materially and thematically. In this way, hybridised figures can be used to explore the estranged subjectivity on the screen. Besides, the integration of live action and animation is used as a way to estrange existing aesthetic styles, such as cartoon's hyperrealism.

0.2 Methods and Methodologies

This section explains the methodology used and how it established interaction between my live-action/animated practice and its contextual and theoretical positioning.

A major purpose of research is to create new knowledge that "increases our awareness of whom we are and about the world in which we live" (Sullivan 2005: 73). In this sense practice and theory together could consummate the research engagement since "to know" means to be able to think and act and thereby to change things. The problem is how to interweave them meaningfully. The methodology used herein aims to establish a constructive relationship between practice and theory for the emergence of ideas and the re-conceptualisation of working methods.

Contextual review (including literature review, case study, and synthesis of my previous works) is used in the development of practices, and the making of practice (along with documentation, reflection in and after the making process) is used to embody, test and push existing understandings. Practice and theory are carried out alternately so that they can be interwoven conceptually and physically. Cyclic strategy constitutes the basic framework of the research process. As described in the previous section, the research questions and the early arguments of the thesis are framed around both making and positioning the first practice of this study, *Nothing to Do with Weather*. The arguments are constructed through the process of answering research questions, which are gradually reshaped and in response to the practices and commentary texts (made up of practice documentation, self-analysis, and analysis of context) in a cyclic research process.

Due to the multi-dimensional characteristic of the combination of live action and animation, a wide range of literature is referenced to reassess its function and implications. In this section the body of literature is introduced under four headings: "the uncanny and a formalist approach", "moving image as aesthetic experience", "moving image as cultural experience", and "moving image as philosophical inquiry". These categories are used to explain how I located the moving image in different fields of knowledge. For the actual research process, this study began with film and animation theories, including definitions of early cinema, definitions of what constitute of live-action cinema, and literature about animation that is testing and working with mainstream cinema's definitions (for the most part, examined during the Prior Stage in the cyclic process). The function of the integration was then re-considered with reference to Freud's notion of the uncanny, where the effect of estrangement was encountered and further explored (in Cycle A). The idea of estrangement is strongly related to Russian formalist Victor Shklovsky's concepts in “Art as Device” (1917).

However, instead of limiting the idea of estrangement in a conventional formalist sense, I tried to keep it open by looking at its link with Freud’s uncanny and re-addressing it with reference to some Taoist ideas, hoping to provide an understanding which is nourished by both ancient and cross-cultural ideas. Through these concepts the conceptual and physical aspects of the integration become co-dependent. The physical manifestations of the integration incorporate questions raised about its meaning in terms of aesthetic, cultural, and philosophical dimensions. These theories simultaneously affect different approaches to considering and understanding the integration of live action and animation. The main theories and theorists consulted in this study are introduced in this section.

Three practices were produced during the research process: *Nothing to Do with Weather* (Practice A, completed in 2009), *Animating Animator the Animated* (Practice B, completed in 2011), and *Flying Tunes* (Practice C, completed in 2012). Through the use of different research tools, an account of the features of integration emerged along with the body of practice, its documentation and contextualisation. As a practice-led research, I hope the exploration of the operation and meaning of their integration has generated knowledge “grounded in the praxis of human engagement” and yielded outcomes that “can be seen to be individually liberating and culturally enlightening” (Sullivan 2005: 74).

Cyclic Strategy

An extensive variety of methods was used to combine practice and research in other projects. As Kroll (2008: 5) points out, “[s]tudio practice supported by notebooks, journals, etc. could provide raw data … then used by the researcher to exemplify, interrogate, or amplify practice.” Nevertheless they would never be sufficient. The result is usually a lack of economy in reporting, as well as a relative lack of rigour. To remedy this weakness, Dick (1999) suggests the application of dialectic approaches – emphasising the use of brief and multiple research cycles. At each cycle the researcher collects multiple data sets, and then interprets the data by focussing on the agreements and disagreements within the two or more data sets and compares this to prior interpretation. Adapted from Dick’s idea, my research process is defined as a cyclic process formed of four stages: prior stage, Cycle A, Cycle B and Cycle C, which is visualised in fig. 0-2.

In terms of the relationship between practice and research, Bruce Archer (1995: 9) has distinguished between “research about practice”, “research for the purpose of practice”, and “research through practice”. Andrew Taylor (2006), however, designates only two kinds of approaches:

extrinsic/prior and intrinsic/formal research. In this project, contextual studies in the prior stage are composed of "research about practice" and "research for the purpose of practice" in Archer's sense. It belongs at the same time to Taylor's extrinsic/prior research, where the exploration is carried out into subject matter and into what has an independent existence external to the practice. The following three cycles then activate the intrinsic/formal research type through embracing the practical exploration and extension of pre-existing forms or concepts, and the formulation of new ones. During the process of filmmaking, there is also an accompanying extrinsic study inspired by the hands-on process. Both kinds of methods work together, with one prompting the other. In this sense, all the three types of relationship in Archer's sense were contained in each of the cycles.

To sum up, the cyclic process (containing Prior Stage, Cycle A, Cycle B and Cycle C) begins with exploring extrinsic materials/texts and getting a general idea of how thinkers and practitioners in film and animation discipline understand the relationship between live action and animation. Rudimentary answers and arguments are yielded in the early cycle and used to refine both questions and methods for later cycles. The process and content are successively refined at each cycle, and a set of comparatively stable argument is reached in the end of the research. The whole process is explained in detail below.

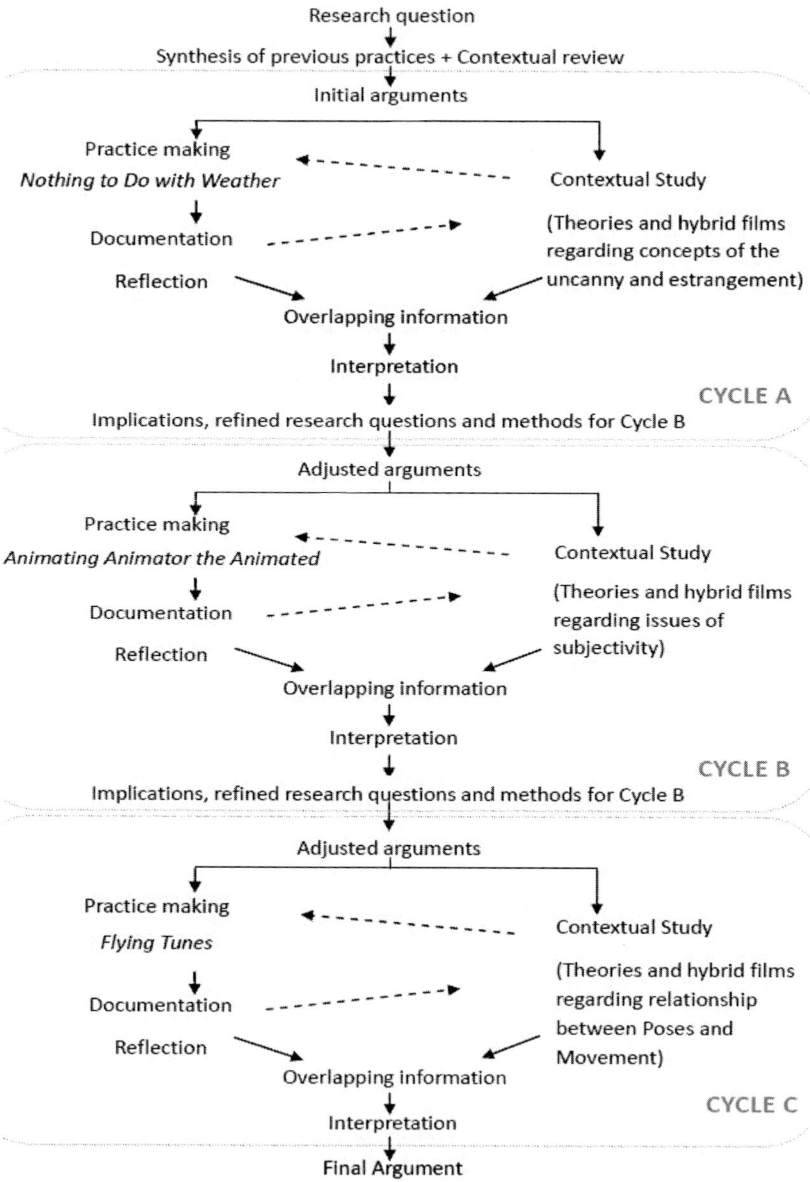

Fig. 0-2: Research Cycles

Prior stage

In the prior stage, I explored my research interests, and made initial arguments. I reviewed articles, papers and a body of historical hybrid films in relation tothe dialectic relationship between live action and animation. I also examined my previous practices and thought about their implications. In this stage I recognised that, instead of a harmonised or seamless integration between live action and animation, it was the tension and discordance I intended to explore. The study in this stage formed my interpretation of live action and animation as an opposing pair, as discussed in Chapter 1.

A script for the first practice, *Nothing to Do with Weather*, was then conceived in order to get hands-on experience in testing the visual effect of various ways of integrating live action and animation. The first practice plan was carried out afterward in Cycle A. A cyclic process thus began.

Cycle A

As described in the "Research Questions" section, along with the making of *Nothing to Do with Weather*, the initial arguments were modified, and the research questions were formed during this stage. This first practice, although based on my illustrated diary for the first year studying aboard, was an expressive work carried out quite freely, aiming to gain some idea of my ability to handle diverse filmmaking techniques. I kept a diary and documented the inspirations and in-action reflections that occurred through the process. After the creative process ended and the first work was displayed in an exhibition, I pondered on the documentation created during it, and wrote up retrospective reviews.

As previously described, this practice was developed around the idea of creating a piece of work that could demonstrate as many examples as possible of the integration between live action and animation. Also discussed previously was how this attempt echoed an experience of in-between two states, and led me to focus on theories about the uncanny and Shklovsky's Russian formalism. Together they formed the basis of my understanding of estrangement, as delineated in Chapter 2. While most of the discussion of the impact of digital tools seems to focus on their ability to conceal the contrast between live action and animation, I wished to explore their ability in a different way; and the idea of estrangement became an interpretive tool for me to endow the operation of material with meaning. At the end of this stage I identified the effect of estrangement as a core notion for my subsequent practice, where the integration of pixilation and cartoon's hyperrealism became the centre of my technical exploration.

Cycle B

This cycle was the longest and most complicated, in which I encountered various technical challenges in practice and came up with numerous ideas in writing. The bulk of the time and effort went into two things: experimenting with how to integrate pixilation and cartoon's hyperrealism, and developing a story which could make this integration a way to demonstrate my idea of estrangement.

In terms of the technical experiment, I planned to first produce several pieces of hand-drawn animation, and then, with the help of stop-motion software, ask a live actor to act the animated sequences out frame by frame (as explained in Chapter 4). I planned to shoot the pixilation performance in front of a green screen so that the pixilated result could be combined with a virtual background. Therefore, at this stage I studied green-screen methods (e.g. Jackman 2007), compared various ways of chroma keying using After Effects, and carried out several tests both at home and at the University's Studio. For a practical knowledge of character animation, I consulted books by Culhane (1988), Thomas & Johnston (1981), Whitaker & Halas (1981), and Williams (2001). I produced five pieces of hand-drawn animation sequences, including around one thousand drawings (including those discarded). I decided to be the live actor myself because, as it was still in the early phase of testing, the shooting process would encounter occasional technical problems, and I was the one who would be available at any time. Besides, the method of making pixilation with stop-motion software was time-consuming and exhausting and it was very difficult to find a volunteer to be the actor.

In terms of story and script development, the main aim was to make the narrative and the technical application meaningful for each other. Initially I had an idea about how a fly suggests a growing feeling between a man and a woman. I kept making and re-making the script around this idea. As a result, there were four versions of the same story, but none of them seemed ideal for the pixilated sequences produced at this stage. I therefore decided to temporarily abandon this story and started a whole new one: *Animating Animator the Animated* (2'47"), which became Practice B.

This story is about the animator's subjectivity, about animating and being animated, manipulating and being manipulated. This theme, although it clearly related to my life and creative experiences at that time, only became fully articulated and conscious when I was trying to sum up my understandings of historical hybrid films in different eras. I found that subjectivity was one of the major themes highlighted by the integration of live action and animation in those films. Moreover, an estranged subjectivity could be a good way to reflect on a common feeling in our digital era. The construction of subjectivity in hybrid films became the subject of Chapter 3.

Although it took much time and effort, the result of the technical experiment in integrating pixilation and cartoon's hyperrealism in this cycle did not match my expectations (as mentioned in Chapter 4), so prompted further technical experiments in the next cycle. The story abandoned at this stage was continued, with modifications, and filmed/animated in the next cycle and became Practice C, *Flying Tunes*.

Cycle C

Flying Tunes (8'27") is the longest work in this project. Its title references the Warner Bros. classical cartoon series "Looney Tunes" (1930-1969) because the caricaturised performance presented in *Flying Tunes* was aiming for the crazy funniness of the "Looney Tunes". I also used sound effects and melodies extracted from "Looney Tunes" in *Flying Tunes* to indicate their connection.

Apart from aiming to develop an improved integration of pixilation and cartoon's hyperrealism based on the experience acquired in Cycle B, this third practice also experimented with combining different kinds of performance style: naturalistic, stage, and cartoonal performances. In addition, through the integration of live actors and CGI background, the tension between live action's naturalism and CGI animation's photorealism would emerge. The final script for this practice was developed around the idea of the double and the inexplicable behaviour in people's lives that hopefully would make the above technical strategies meaningful in producing the effect of estrangement. All these contributed to the discussions in Chapter 2 and 3, where the issues of estrangement and subjectivity are examined. Yet the technical experiment with producing cartoony pixilation had led to an inquiry into the relationship between poses and movement, which became the subject of Chapter 4.

Use of Theory/ Main Theorists

The theories consulted in this research are categorised and introduced under four groupings: the uncanny and a formalist approach, moving image as aesthetic experience, moving image as cultural experience, and moving image as philosophical inquiry. These are not exclusive categories defined in a strict sense. Aesthetics, for example, is often considered as a branch of philosophy dealing with the nature of art. This categorisation is simply used to illustrate how I located the moving image in different fields of knowledge, and how the research topic was accessed from various perspectives.

The uncanny and a formalist approach

In understanding the idea of estrangement, the following texts are considered central resources in this research: Freud's "The Uncanny" (1919), Shklovsky's "Art as Technique" (1917), Nicholas Royle's *The Uncanny* (2003) and Carlo Ginzburg's essay "Making it Strange" in *Wooden Eye: Nine Reflections on Distance* (2001).

When thinking about the method of making practice, beyond the consideration of tools, materials and techniques, etc., there are other fundamental methods regarding the work's purpose and function, something that may make a practice "art". As for the question of what art is, Shklovsky (1956[1917]: 11) regards the main element of art as estrangement: he states that "the purpose of art is to impart the sensation of things as they are perceived and not as they are known". Harold Bloom (1994: 2) reckons that "[o]ne mark of an originality that can win canonical status for a literary work is a strangeness that we either never altogether assimilate, or that becomes such a given that we are blinded to its idiosyncrasies". Royle (2003: 15) links Bloom's "strangeness" with Freud's uncanny and lead me to the connection between uncanny and Shklovsky's formalist standpoint. Ginzburg (2001: 1-24) understands estrangement in connection with the riddle when he traces the Russian formalist notion of de-familiarization back to Marcus Aurelius' *Meditations*, and then to the lore of the folk riddle. I draw on these ideas in my account of the effects of the integration, and suggest that a formalist approach actually enacts a bridge between my technical and thematic concerns. The use of these related concepts is understood as a metaphor to expand technical issues into the implications of content and the narrative, and place the concerns of filmmaking into the area of visual culture.

Moving image as aesthetic experience

Manovich's *The Language of New Media* (2001) talks at length about the changing states of the interface between live action and animation under the influence of digital technology. Its analysis provides a starting point for this research. The discussions on montage and digital compositing (Manovich 2001: 136-160) are especially pertinent to my speculation about the integration of live action and animation.

Discussions about stitching together pieces of film have long been an integral part of film theory. Significant texts include Sergei Eisenstein's montage theory (Eisenstein 1992; 1998), classical editing theory (Bordwell& Thompson 2010; Giannetti 2011), and the suture theory (Bordwell 1985; Butte 2008; Oudart 1978). While looking like similar devices, they emphasise very different functions and aspects. Eisenstein's notion of montage is "a *collision* … of two factors [that] gives rise to an idea' (Eisentein 1998: 87); the classical editing strategy is about continuity, and about telling stories efficiently; the suture theory is about "creating gaps and then filling them", about the "Absent One" (Bordwell 1985: 111), and is often a topic in meditations on the representation of subjectivity in film narrative (as presented in Butt 2008). Although they mainly focus on editing and the arrangement of camera, they are all suggestive of the juxtaposition of heterogeneous elements between shots or within a shot.

In processing the research questions, I was inspired by a range of theoretical works on early cinema, the nature of animation, classical cinema and new media. Tom Gunning (1989: 1995) was one of the first scholars to look at the reliance on spectacle and special effects of early and silent films. Although the academic research of animation is still marginal compared to film studies, the texts of Donald Crafton (1993), Paul Wells (1998), and Esther Leslie (2002) constitute comprehensive understandings of animation's nature and capacities. They are illuminating in terms of understanding animation's subversive characteristics in contrast to live-action cinema. Shilo McClean's *Digital Storytelling* (2007) and Dan North's *Performing Illusions* (2008) discuss the roles of digital visual effects in filmmaking. North's text emphasises special effects' function of subverting the integrity of cinematic image's relation to its referent. McClean, on the other hand, claims that while greatly expanding the possibilities for contemporary filmmaking, the use of digital visual effects remains simply a set of tools in the service of classical storytelling. Along with David Bordwell's and Kristin Thompson's standard textbook on the analysis of cinema *Film Art: An Introduction* (2010), McClean's text provides an understanding of the function of special effects from the perspective of classical filmmaking.

Jay David Bolter's and Richard Grusin's *Remediation* (1999) was one of the first academic works that describes new media as a genre with unique aesthetic markings. Lev Manovich's *The Language of New Media* (2001) and Andrew Darley's *Visual Digital Culture: Surface play and Spectacle in New Media Genres* (2000) offer some rigorous and far-reaching theorisation on this subject. They both emphasise new media's historical continuity with pre-existing forms, and at the same time, the need to understand new media on its own terms. Although presenting different concerns, they have both worked on mapping the aesthetics of new media, including digital imaging, which is central to my study.

Moving image as cultural experience

My consideration of how to account for the meaning of the interfaces between live action and animation was influenced by some of the ideas in Fredric Jameson's *Postmodernism and Cultural Theories* (1989) and *Postmodernism, or, The Cultural Logic of Late Capitalism* (1991), where he analyses culture as a historical and social phenomenon alongside economic production and distribution or political power relationships. From this point of view, it is necessary to perceive the key elements of the production of artistic objects within its social context.

In respect to considering visual production within the social/cultural context, Jonathan Crary's *Techniques of the Observer* (1992), Andrew Darley's *Visual Digital Culture* (2000) and Dan North's *Performing Illusions* (2008) provide plenty of cues. Crary's text is about vision and its historical construction before 1850, and is working at a redefinition of the relations between modernity, modernism and spectatorship. Darley's text explores the relationship between digital technologies and existing media, and considers the effects of these new image forms on the experience of visual culture. North's text situates cinematic effects in the cultural lineage of the stage performers and illusionists of the nineteenth century. They all highlight the notion that art is a social phenomenon that should be understood within the historical development and the specificity of social context.

Crary (1992: 1) has noted that the formalization and diffusion of computer-generated imagery have brought "the ubiquitous implantation of fabricated visual "spaces" radically different from the mimetic capacities of film, photography, and television". Indeed the intervention of digital technology is one of the hot topics in the territory of cultural history and criticism. There have been debates among cultural commentators on a sense of change in the character of cultural/aesthetic practices from around 1960s onwards, where a perceived shift seemed to be under way in the general experience of culture (particularly in the developed countries of the West). Either it is understood as a new phase of modernism itself ("late" or "later modernism"), or a move to something altogether different (so-called "postmodernism"), the idea of a shift in cultural and aesthetic practices is widely acknowledged. For example, Darley (2000) indicates that some new features are now so prevalent as to constitute a new and significant dimension of representation within it. By looking at the works of Jean Baudrillard (whose thinking was influenced by the work of Walter Benjamin and Marshall McLuhan), Umberto Eco and Fredric Jameson, Darley (2000: 58-77) introduces a host of related terms such as reproducibility and repetition, self-referentiality and intertextuality, simulation and pastiche, and superficiality and spectacle. These have been used with cultural and aesthetic connotations as concepts to explain and describe practices, processes, forms and conditions within contemporary visual culture.

To be seen as a part of cultural experience, the function and meaning of the interface is re-located in the light of its past and present manifestations in filmmaking. Although the cultural aspect is not the main part of this study, all arts including films are a kind of cultural production and should be more or less evaluated in terms of their cultural implications. This perspective is applied throughout Chapter 2, 3 and 4. In this respect, the combination of live action and animation can be considered as representing both the relationship between different modes of reality and the status of modernity.

Moving image as philosophical inquiry

I use aspects of post-stucturalist philosophy to consider the complexity of the duality between live action and animation. Ideas in Derrida's discourses (especially *Positions* in 1981) and Gilles Deleuze's & Felix Guattari's *A Thousand Plateaus* (1987) provide basic standpoints in reflecting on the functions and implications of the differences between the two.

Through contemporary animation studies, especially essays in the two volumes of *The Illusions of Life* edited by Alan Cholodenko (in 1997 and 2007), post-structuralist articulations of the world are transferred and associated with the notions of animation, of cinema, and of the live-action/animated hybrids. Together they not only support my understanding of the opposed but supplemental tendencies within cinema, but also enable a way of thinking about moving image's relation to the concept of the uncanny where desire, in the act of making it strange, is affected. In this sense then, the interface between live action and animation in my account is characterised by its uncanniness, which is effective in summoning up the constructedness beneath the figuration on the screen.

Moreover, by offering insights into the cinematic ideas of time and movement, Henri Bergson's *The Creative Mind* and Deleuze's *Cinema 1: The Movement-Image* (1986) form a crucial part of the foundation for my account on the gap between pixilation and cartoon's hyperrealist style. Mata Braun's *Picturing Time: Work of Etienne-Jules Marey* was consulted for his inspiring comparison between Bergson and Marey (1830-1904). My experiments in film-making practice elicit questions about the representations of time and movement in moving image. By referring to philosophical concepts, I am able to develop my own interpretation and devise a correspondent strategy, in which different codes of representation are integrated with the application of digital tools, and a hybridisation with new meanings is produced. In this case the interface has a role to play in the understanding of the constructed nature of cinematic time. As the result, the investigation of materiality and meaning inevitably involves exploration in a philosophical sense.

0.3 Structure of Thesis

Being the source and result of these themes as expressed in the written thesis, the practical component of this thesis submission consists of three films: *Nothing to Do with Weather* (Practice A), *Animating Animator the Animated* (Practice B), and *Flying Tunes* (Practice C). As attempts to create hybrid forms aiming at demonstrating or experimenting with how ideas emerged during the research process, the three practices are included in the body of the text in different ways, as stated below in the description of each chapter.

Exploring the issues to make a new interpretation of the integration of live action and animation and to account for the practice in this research, each chapter of the thesis presents a different approach. Live action and animation are seen as an opposing pair in Chapter 1. Their integrations are then discussed by linking aesthetic and existential estrangement in Chapter 2, by inquiring into the subjectivity of the hybridised figure in Chapter 3, and by collapsing the borders between "the condensation of time" and "the dissection of time" in Chapter 4. The potential of digital tools' ability to intervene in the themes is discussed in each chapter.

Chapter 1 explores the very basis of this study by looking into the characteristics of live action and animation. On the premise that the integration of live action and animation can make moving images more exciting by constantly interrupting each other than by uniting each other, the investigation focuses on the opposing tendencies between them by considering these two as an opposing pair, with their opposing (but not opposed) qualities described in their definitions. The intention is to arrive at a fundamental understanding of how the dialectic relationship could function. In this chapter, the three practices are considered in terms of their technical parameters and operation.

Chapter 2 investigates the notions of the uncanny and estrangement in terms of their relationships to the moving image. Since live action and animation can be supplementary to each other, and their combination could create layered and sometimes conflicting meanings for the hybrid figure, this chapter suggests that the experience of the supplementary can be the bridge linking the uncanny and estrangement. The focus is on finding a different way of understanding the role of aesthetic estrangement in moving image from a Far-East Asian standpoint. In this chapter, all three practices take up the role of interacting with the concept of estrangement. In addition to being part of the experiment to create an effect of estrangement through the operation of materiality, the three practices are to some extent an allegory about the alienation a Far-East Asian filmmaker may feel in a world seemingly dominated by Western paradigms.

Chapter 3 argues that subjectivity is an effective trope for investigating the formal manipulation of the integration between live action and animation. Recognising the importance of personal experience for the subjectivity expressed in the practice, this chapter starts with a discussion of the impact of studying and living abroad on my idea of subjectivity. Through inspecting historical experiments, this chapter shows that the experience in relation to the struggle of subjectivity can be exposed by the objective progressive drive inherent in hybrid works. By exposing the constructedness and dynamic nature of the hybridised figure on the screen, "selfhood" becomes a relationship rather than a fixed essence. In this chapter, the hybridised figures in Practice B and C contribute to showing how the construction of self-identity could be revealed or interrogated by the encounter of live action and animation; while in Practice A the interconnection between photographed and hand-drawn figures provides a display of intersubjectivities between characters.

Chapter 4 contends that there is discordance between pixilation and cartoon's hyperrealism. Thinking about the inter-relationship between poses and movement prompted the question as to whether pixilated and live-action films might belong to two different image systems. This chapter examines the possible borders between the two modes of image system, and considers the strategies for pixilation to approach cartoon's hyperrealism. In this chapter, Practice B and C have a direct and causal relation to the theorisation of ideas. They present different approaches to combining pixilation and the cartoon style. The result in Practice B leads to the development of strategies in Practice C, making it a demonstration of breaking down the distinctions between the condensation and the dissection of time.

Chapter One

Live Action and Animation as an Opposing Pair

Why is it necessary to distinguish between live action and animation? After all, they are of the same breed – they are both simply moving images, illusions that constitute the cinematic world. Yet a "line" between live action and animation does exist. The border between the two has generated discussions about their different natures, roles, functions and statuses in relation to each other. This research argues that there are opposing attributes between live action and animation, and the tensions between them can be a contributing factor in the evolution of the moving image. Digital imaging technology, while often used for its unprecedented capacity for simulation, also has unique ways with which to create alienation effects. Hence, it is also argued in this research that digital imaging technology, instead of erasing distinctions between live action and animation, can be employed to bring out the opposing qualities between them.

Discussing the above arguments, this chapter deals with the two basic concerns of the research: the opposing qualities between live action and animation, and the potential of digital imaging technology to explore the tension between them. What are their opposing attributes? How does their relationship – sometimes dialectic and sometimes supplementary – explain some of the opposed tendencies within the whole of moving imagery? What is the significance of exposing the tension between opposing qualities? The discussion begins with the most basic and straightforward step – the reviewing of definitions – to find the opposites. It will then proceed to discuss the tradition of special effects and their linkage with CGI, and finally, digital technology's capacity to explore inconsistencies within moving image.

1.1 Live Action versus Animation

A common way to think about animation is in relation to live-action media. Being marginalised for most of the twentieth century, animation has been the least theorised area of cinema. Kristen Thompson (1980: 108) states in "Implications of the Cel Animation Technique" that, "Hollywood defined the cartoon by its difference from live-action cinema." However, if we look up the term "live-action" in dictionaries, we would find that in many of them the term does not exist. Even if it is included, the definition is often dependent on that of animation. For example, *The Merriam-Webster Dictionary* (2011) defines "live-action" as: "of, relating to, or featuring cinematography that is not produced by animation." In this dictionary definition, it is through defining "animation" that the definition of "live-action" can be established – the non-exercise of animation. This may be because the term live-action is too specific to appear in a dictionary that is for more general usages, or it may be because that this term has a much shorter history compared with animation (therefore it is defined by animation, a pre-existing term). In any case, this could suggest it is sensible to understand the difference between live action and animation by accessing animation first.

Many have attempted to define or describe animation. One example is Charles Solomon. Examining a variety of techniques he regards as animation, Solomon (1989: vii) considers that there are two factors that link those different media, and can serve as the basis for a workable definition of animation. They are: (1) the imagery is recorded frame-by-frame and (2) the illusion of motion is created, rather than recorded.

Another example is Edward S. Small's and Eugene Levinson's succinct claim in 1989 that animation is "the technique of single-frame cinematography" (Small & Levinson 1989: 73). The "frame by frame" criterion seems to be a fundamental dividing line between animation and live action. However, there are also some who refuse to use the "frame by frame" criterion as a fundamental definition for animation. Pierre Hebert (2005: 182), for example, views it as "a definition more for animators than for directors", and that "it is responsible for the general weakness of aesthetics in the field of animation". For Hebert, what matters most is animation's relationship with live action, an intricate relationship that originates from animation's and live action's respective connections to their common origin. He states:

> The invention of cinema is at the meeting point of two different vectors of technical development: photography and the pre-cinema motion games popular during the nineteenth century. It resulted in this principle of

> capturing and reproducing motion through a series of discrete images driven by a mechanical device. For live action cinema, once this mechanical image processor was invented, it readily became a black box that was taken for granted, unquestioned, a totally neutral ground beneath the level where artistic decision-making was taking place. One the contrary, animation is constantly reopening the technical black box (Hebert 2005: 183).

It appears that for Hebert animation is more about being reflexive, disenchanting and enlightening. However, if one thinks about the "illusion of life", a phrase often used by classic animation artists to describe the essence of animation, it seems that animation is greatly concerned with the endowment of life, something that is more about magic than disenchantment. As explained by Disney animation masters Frank Thomas and Ollie Johnson (1981), the creation of the "illusion of life" is fundamental for audience involvement. John Lasseter (1994) summarises their notion and claims, "[c]haracter animation isn't the fact that an object looks like a character or has a face or hands", rather, it is "when an object moves like it is alive."

Like classic animators, Alan Cholodenko, a scholar who has tried to revisit animation theory from a more philosophical approach, also believes the fascination with animated cartoons is a fascination with the illusion of life (Cholodenko 1991: 20). For Cholodenko, the illusion of life is a crucial subject of speculation concerning not just animation but *all* cinematic apparatus. This might be true if we consider the ambiguity between the conventional distinctions between cinema's realism and illusionism. Those theorists or pioneering filmmakers who were concerned with cinema's faithful reproduction of pre-existing reality in a conventional sense have been re-interpreted and re-considered by more recent theorists. Film scholar Adam Lowenstein (2007: 57) considers Bazin's "The Ontology of Photographic Image" is actually a version of surrealism. His essay argues that Bazin's "realism" frequently moves toward the territory of surrealism. Another intriguing case is Louis Lumière. His name is often associated with documentary and access to unmediated reality. According to a widespread belief, when Lumière's *The Arrival of a Train at La Ciotat Station* was first shown in 1895, the audience was so overwhelmed by the moving image of a life-sized train coming directly at them that people screamed and rushed from the auditorium. However, some scholars have doubted the veracity of this incident, and considered that the Lumières were actually perceived as magicians by their contemporaries, not as realists (Gunning 1990: 96). Gunning (1990: 96) suggests "the fascination and even the realism of early films related more strongly to the traditions of magic theatre (with its presentation of popular science as spectacle) than to later conceptions of documentary realism". The "real" possessed by photographic images was just as illusory as drawn pictures. They were both images captured by the film negative. The main difference between photographic and graphic/drawn images is that the former indicates a tangible world which has once been in front of the lens.

However, this is a crucial difference. In the past, live-action film was synonymous with cinema; the basic gesture of cinema was to open the shutter and start the film rolling, and record whatever happens in front of the lens. Although there were great varieties of styles in cinema, they were all "children of machine vision" (Manovich 2001: 307). The symbol of the machine eye informs the realistic aesthetic tradition of cinema. For Andre Bazin, photography's most unique capability is to capture an image automatically, "without the creative invention of man" (2005, 13). Similarly, Siegfried Kracauer argued that "Film … is uniquely equipped to record and reveal physical reality and, hence, gravitates toward it" (Kracauer 1960: 28). Even the non-realist Eisenstein found the shot to be a "photo-fragment of nature" (Prince 2004: 26). Such arguments reflect the difficulty of modifying recorded images before the digital age, which lent live action "value as document, assuring its authenticity" (Manovich 2001: 307).

Often starting with a blank piece of paper, what distinguishes animation from live action is that an animation artist has the obligation (or freedom) to make extremely detailed decisions about their character's shapes and forms. For Disney animators, although live-action footage was a gold mine for studying personality and performance, there was nothing in the films that could be copied or used just the way it was. Thomas and Johnson (1981: 323) explain, "The camera certainly records what is there, but it records *everything* that is there, with an impartial lack of emphasis. On the other hand, an artist shows what he sees is there, especially that which might not be perceived by others. His drawings can be closer to the true realism of an object because he can be selective and personal in what he chooses to show".

Looking at animation in this way, the difference between live action and animation is obvious. If the symbol of the machine eye represents live action, then it would be the artist's hand that stands for animation. Walter Benjamin describes the advent of photography in his influential article "The Work of Art in the Age of Mechanical Reproduction" (written in 1935): "For the first time in the process of pictorial reproduction, photography freed the hand of the most important artistic functions which henceforth developed only upon the eye looking into a lens. Since the eye perceives more swiftly than the hand can draw, the process of pictorial reproduction was acceleration so enormously that it could keep pace with speech" (Benjamin 1992: 213). Photography facilitated the efficiency of visual reproduction in a massive and unprecedented way.

Supposing the technique of photography had not been invented, and there was no live-action film, would a form of cinematic apparatus for public projection have developed? One could say that Emile Reynaud's Théâtre Optique (patented in 1892) is an exemplification, even though it projected drawings, not photographs. An illustration (fig. 1-1) shows that a large mass of people would watch the performance at the same time. Although lacking records of the number of persons attending each show, it is said that from 1882 to 1900, the year it closed, over 500,000 people had seen it (Saerens 1997). Developed from the simple and looped Zoetrope, the Théâtre Optique could create a twelve- or fifteen-minutes continuous projection. By using spools to feed and take-up the extended picture band, one work might involve more than 600 painstakingly drawn images on a 140-feet ribbon (Naughton 1999). The size of the work is huge, but what was more astonishing is the labour demanded, the artistry required, and the skill needed to illustrate the nuance between adjacent drawings without the assistance of modern animating equipment such as a tracing box or tracing paper. The very craftsmanship characterised by Reynaud's invention characterises the popular view of animation even in the contemporary era.

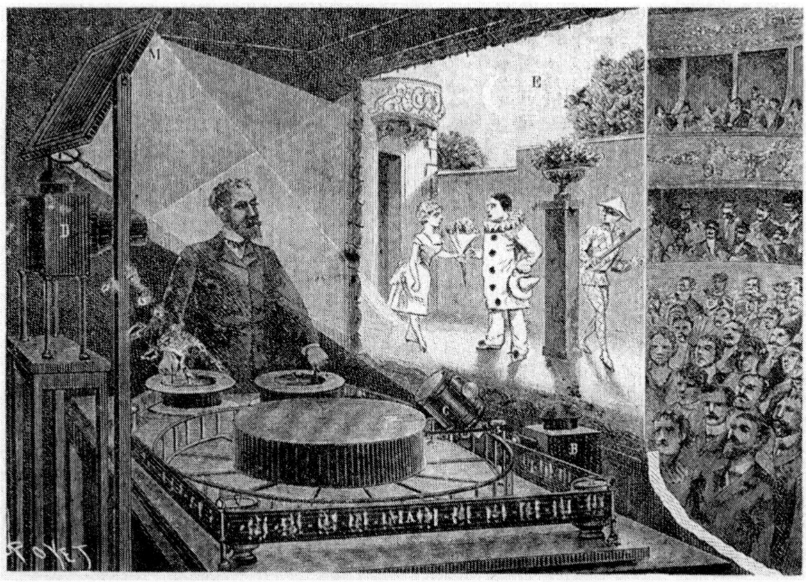

Fig 1-1: The Théâtre Optique and its inventor Emile Reynaud (1844-1918) with a scene from Pauvre Pierro. Illustrated by Louis Poyet (1846-1919).

In this sense, the image of the artist's hand speaks to a lot of animation artists' active engagement. No wonder scholars would see animation as a mark of the return of the artist as a source and origin of the image, and take it as a purer artistic form (e.g. Elsaesser 1998: 206; MacGillivray 1007: 1). As a result, there is a contrast between live action's inclination tonaturalism and animation's value as personal or stylistic expression. A poetic description of animation's opposition to live action is made by novelist Steven Millhauser:

> The animated cartoon was a far more honest expression of the cinematic illusion than the so-called realistic (live-action) film, because the cartoon revelled in its own illusory nature, exulted in the impossible – indeed it claimed the impossible as its own, exalted it as its own highest end, found in impossibility, in the negation of the actual, its profoundest reason for being (Millhauser 1998: 107).

Because of this contrast, although the digital seems to have brought animation back to the centre of the stage, when computer animation made its first forays into the cinema, its forms were considerably neutralised by the naturalist tradition of live action film that claimed its prerogative rights over animation (Farley 2003: 4).

The contrast between the images of the machine eye and the artist's hand not only demonstrates the artist's role, but also concerns material inquiry. At the most basic level, live action films are the "children of a recording process that uses lenses, regular sampling of time, and photographic media" (Manovich 2001: 307). This comment seems to speak to two basic qualities of the materiality of live-action film: photographicness and real-time recording. In a broader sense, real-time recording can be considered to be any kind of regular sampling of time; and the photographicness can be taken as any kind of imprint, such as fossils, finger prints or maybe lime-scale in a kettle, as long as it is a fixed, framed, unmediated evidence of the past.

In terms of being an intermediary instrument between observer and world, afilm camera has a lot in common with the camera obscura that was prevalent in seventeenth- and eighteenth-century Europe. The structural principles of the two devices are not related, but they both, to some degree, share the myth that it is possible and necessary to escape the uncertainties of mere human vision and the confusions of the senses to gain an objective understanding of the world. As described by Crary (1992), for two hundred years the camera obscura existed as a philosophical metaphor, as a model of how observation leads to truthful inferences about the world. Being synonymous with the production of truth, a decisive function of the camera obscura was "to sunder the act of seeing from the physical body of the observer, to decorporealize vision" (1992: 39). The dominance of the camera obscura metaphor, as pointed out by Crary (1992: 29-32), ended abruptly atthe beginning of the nineteenth century when a new kind of "realism" started to form its philosophical paradigm.

The science of vision began to mean an inquiry into "the physiological makeup of the human subject", rather than just "the mechanics of light and optical transmission" (Crary 1992: 70). In this period mass visual culture was highly dependent on the priority of models of "subjective vision", in contrast to the model of the camera obscura's suppression of subjective vision. Distinct from being the idea of a vision that is unique to artists, here the notion of "subjective vision", as Crary (1992:16) states, refers to a vision that is "taken out of the incorporeal relations of the camera obscura and relocated in the human body". Using the models of subjective vision, a number of optical toys were invented and became popular in the nineteenth century. For example, according to Crary (1992: 16), the Phenakistiscope was produced as a part of the empirical study of retinal afterimages, and the Stereoscope was developed as an effort to quantify and formalise the physiological operation of binocular vision. Subjective vision in the empirical sense is bound up with non-veridical theories of vision that are also indispensible to the birth of modern animation.

Animation is an art based on illusions of specific movement through the suspension of automatic recording. It tends to interrogate the gap between what an audience sees and what it perceives. In doing so, an animator appeals to "the psycho-physiological motion perception mechanisms" (Graca 2006: 1; MacGillivray 2007: 1). The psychophysical perception aspects are therefore essential to understanding animation, and in drawing a line between live action and animation. As such, it seems animation inherits a great deal from nineteenth-century optical devices in terms of the exploration of psychophysical perception, the disclosure of material fabrication, and the play of hallucination on a frame-by-frame basis.

Photography however seems to extend the metaphor of the camera obscura in recreating the fiction that the "objective" and "free" subject was still viable. From an early formation such as the Kinematoscope, the prototype of the cinematographic device had basically been a cabinet box with filmstrips inside. Along with the "dark room" which was indispensible for developing images on negatives, cinematography was metaphorically becoming a "black box" of technology. Ironically, while concealing and mystifying the "reproduction of truth" in a black box, the invention of the camera also in a sense "enlightened" animation: photography's immediacy provided a dissection of real action for animators in terms of the analysis and reconstruction of movement frame by frame. One of the famous examples is Eadweard Muybridge's Zoogyroscope in the 1870s. His work is the study of motion in photography by using a succession of snapshots to decompose and recompose the movements of human beings and animals. It has informed numerous animation pioneers and is still a sort of bible for animators today (Williams 2001: 328).

The above discussion shows that animation is at the same time the illusion of life and the disenchantment of the technical black box. It also shows that sometimes live action and animation are like two obviously different entities, while sometimes the demarcation between them seems ambiguous and unnecessary. This simply underlines the dynamic mutuality between live action and animation. It seems they are an opposing pair, but their opposites are built and disentangled simultaneously. The relation between live action and animation is thus often one of negation or supplementation. There is a constantly changing tension between them, which is what this study intends to explore.

In *Nothing to Do with Weather*, the first practice of this project, for most of the scenes the photographs are not mixed with drawings. Yet it does not mean that live action and animation are similarly separated. The photographic world within the film is made using the stop-frame technique that imbues the live-action material with the quality of the animated. The stop-frame photography abandons real-time recording's smoothness and spontaneity. The figure in it is jiggly, hobbled and sometimes out of kilter, an awkward presence that will cause the viewer to feel there is something not quite right. Without harmonising the opposed tendencies within the moving image, the stop-frame-photographic figuration – the results are commonly known as pixilated figures – is a combination of live action and animation that tends to manifest tension between this opposing pair. This tension is significant for experimental films. As for the creation of such tension, I would suggest it may lie in the contrast between the establishment and disturbance of "perceptual realism". Here "perceptual realism" refers to the concept introduced by Stephen Prince in 1996, considered by many other scholars as having opened up the discussion of filmic realism and reducing the divide between digital film practice and realist film theory (Surman 2003: 18-21; North 2008: 21-22). Prince states:

> A perceptually realistic image is one which structurally corresponds to human audiovisual experience of three-dimensional space. Perceptual realistic images correspond to this experience because filmmakers build them to do so. Such images display a nested hierarchy of cues which organise the display of light, colour, texture, movement, and sound in ways that correspond with the viewer's understanding of these phenomena in daily life. Perceptual realism, therefore, designates a relationship between the image or film and the spectator, and it can encompass both unreal

> images and those which are referentially realistic. Because of this, unreal images may be referentially fictional but perceptually realistic (Prince 1996: 32).

Although Prince's discussion focuses mainly on digital images, it is also pertinent to other kinds of visual media. As Surman (2003: 19) comments, "whatever the media, be it CGI, photography or animation, the way in which it puts forward perceptual cues is central to the creation of filmic realism". Perceptual realism here can be seen as the unifying of different elements for a plausible world, no matter what style it is. In this sense, it can be understood as the harmonisation of live-action and animated elements. The establishment of perceptual realism is necessary for the viewer's involvement. However, to reveal the "hand" behind the scene, a certain amount of disturbance is useful. The two together can induce tension between live action and animation, and encourage an interpretive attitude in the viewer.

The tension between establishing and disturbing perceptual realism is crucial not just for experimental works. It is also significant and detectable in mainstream films that emphasise the application of special effects. The idea of creating strikingly "real" characters and placing them seamlessly into an apparently three-dimensional world has become almost a commonplace of contemporary digital cinema. Spectacle in mainstream cinema seems in principle to demand an attitude of passive acceptance. However, North (2008: 6) argues that the spectator of these illusionist films is actually "active in making sense of it as a technical accomplishment", rather than simply passive in receiving it as "an incomprehensible, overwhelmingly "magical" conjuration". For North (2008: 4-5), special effects can always "be perceived by their mechanical idiosyncrasies or deficiencies, by inadequacies of their manufacture, or by simple acknowledgement of impossibility"; these are not failings of technology but are the "point of access for the spectator's critical engagement with the film on a technical level". He therefore believes that special effects can function as interventions between image and referent, and "break down the blind trust that the viewer has been conditioned to place in the film, and, by extension, all visual media" (North 2008: 23).

Special effects are perhaps the most common way of integrating live action and animation in the history of the moving image (McClean 2008: 6).Today's computer-generated imagery is, to a large extent, seen as part of the Effects tradition. Before discussing digital imaging technology in terms of its potential to induce tension between live action and animation, I would like to continue discussion some historical grounding of special effects, since they both share the goal of allowing the audience to suspend their disbelief while they are watching animated elements.

1.2 Linking Traditional Special Effects and Contemporary CGI

First pioneered by American filmmaker Willis O'Brien (1886-1963) and developed much further with Ray Harryhausen (b. 1920), a "realistic-oriented" stop-motion animation was developed in order to blend well with the live-action background, and to create the illusion of a real-world fantasy. It tends to be a sophisticated version of object animation – more photorealistic in appearance and more naturalistic in movement. It is often called "model animation" (Harryhausen 2008). Model animation has seldom been taken seriously by film scholars, and rarely discussed in the animation academic sphere since it is neither orthodox nor experimental enough (Telotte 2010: 41; Wells 2002: 52). According to the definition of animation mentioned earlier in this chapter – an illusion of movement created frame-by-frame – this approach certainly belongs to the family of animation. However, as Wells (2002: 52) notes, it has often been "absorbed within the Effects tradition rather than receiving recognition in its own right as animation". Telotte (2010: 41), who has focused on the relationship of animation and space, considers the ambiguity of its kinship as a consequence of "its very ability to give life to figures within a real space", which makes the real value of this approach seem to "lay in its ability to add another dimension to conventional cinema, to open up a fantastic dimension that live action might not otherwise achieve", so that is often neglected by animation scholars. O'Brien's achievement in characterising the screen monster may remind us of Winsor McCay'sGertie the Dinosaur. This approach actually echoes and enhances the aesthetic ground rules set up by animation pioneer McCay: the consistent concerns of American artists in general for "solidity, pragmatism, and pictorial realism" (Crafton 1982, 135). In this sense, it may be associated with Disney cartoon animation more than that with European puppet animation.

O'Brien started experiments on the hybrid form from the beginning of his career. His *Nippy's Nightmare* (1911) was one of the earliest attempts at combining live actors with stop-motion characters. In 1925, he accomplished a real-world illusion *The Lost World* (directed by Harry O. Hoyt), which became the first feature-length film in the United States to feature "model animation" as the primary special effects. Perhaps the most discussed of O'Brien's works is *King Kong* (1933), in which the screen monster Kong is a character with personality, expressing emotions and motivation. In this film the animation skills are properly integrated into the "beauty and the beast" storyline. The realism O'Brien achieved is not just in the visual effects, but especially in making Kong a believable and an affecting being. Here King Kong is a giant gorilla whose performative realism can be measured against that of real gorillas. Many imaginary creatures in this kind of film do not have a direct real-world reference, but can still be created by extracting properties from different life forms, and then putting them together into a fictional being, such as Hydra and Kraken – both monsters in Greek mythology. Even prehistoric dinosaurs are actually fictional since there are only fossils for scientists to make a guess at their appearance which is still subject to much scientific debate in the contemporary era. In his book *Animated Bestiary*, Wells (2009: 22) mentions the importance of recognisable true animal actions, behaviours and motivation in animated animal narratives. For those cross-species coupling, or made-up monsters, it is especially crucial to provide enough visual clues to link them with real-world animals, so that a convincing illusion can be built. Advances in technology have only enhanced the degree of elaboration, but donot make them different in kind. This is quite obvious in the re-makes of, or sequels to, those old monster hits using digital visual effects. In this respect, there is a consistency between traditional special effects and modern digital effects; and one of the common goals of these monster movies is this perceptual realism mentioned earlier.

Since in judging this kind of hybrid people are especially concerned with realism, its technological requirements particularly need to keep pace with the times to satisfy the audience's critical eye which also evolves over time. This kind of hybridised imagery can be divided into four processes according to the degree of difficulty of its production: (1) effects animation, (2) character animation (non-human being), (3) pseudo-human being and (4) human being.

Effects Animation

The first, effects animation, is about all the elements, such as smoke, fire, water, and other spectacles of nature. Basically they are imitation of real things happening in the real-time/live-action mode. Such techniques emerged very early and were frequently seen in Melies' trick films (such as the smoke and fire in *La Colonne de Feu*, 1899; rain and water in *Le Royaume De Fées*, 1903). Their presence in filmmaking preceded hand-drawn animation. The imagery might not be frame-by-frame simulation but it was usually the result of multiple exposures, matte effects or camera tricks.

In the pre-computer era, one of the entertainments special effects provided derived from the application of substitutes – using things like light, cloth or paper to substitute for fire, river, snow, ice, etc. Even today, computer simulation is so powerful and relatively easy to use; the "substitute" can still offer interesting and creative results. Young artists like American stop-motion filmmaker PES are still zealously exploring this approach. PES's *Western Spaghetti* (2008), for example, re-creates a common spaghetti cooking process by replacing all the ingredients with objects such as tomato pin cushions, rubber bands, Rubik's cubes, post-it notes, and bubble-wrap. Boiling water, spitting oil and spraying salt: all of them are substitutes. Through the substitute, the most ordinary everyday cooking becomes strange and intriguing, as if we had never really seen it before. By means of manipulating materiality, stop motion creates an effect of estrangement in a way very different from what photography does.

Character Animation (Non-human Being)

The second process is character animation without a human character, such as a dragon or monster. They came early in the hybrid attempts – a desire to bring to life fantastic creatures, something that model animation has pursued. This kind of film is consistent with the realist goal. Many such fictional creatures in the pre-digital era such as King Kong, Mighty Joe Young and Kraken the monster, have been re-made by means of computer when they entered the digital era. David Bordwell & Janet Staiger (1985: 258) compare the goal of innovation in film with that in other industries, while engineers in other industries expend effort developing "unbreakable glass" or "lighter alloy", motion picture engineers' goals are guided by canons such as "showmanship, realism, invisibility".

Increased concealment of artifice and semblance of reality are among the goals of the film industry. The standard threshold of acceptance has risen over time. There are of course exceptions. Today many low-budget B movies still try to break the rules and to prove that they can make fun and enjoyable films without expensive and sophisticated CGI effects. As a particular genre, B movies have their fans. In the Golden Age of Hollywood, B movies were identified as films that were intended for distribution as the less-publicised, bottom half of a double feature. In the 1950s, Harryhausen's model animation films actually emerged as popular B movies. They played on the audience's affection for the gritty visual effects in the films, and in reverse they contributed to shaping the B movie as a special genre such as we know it today.

Film industries outside Hollywood may sometimes possess different set of rules. One example is Tokusatsu – Japanese live-action film or television drama that feature superheroes and make considerable use of special effects. Having a kinship with Japanese theatre, Tokusatsu began to take shape from the early 1950s. Inspired by Hollywood's *King Kong*,

Godzilla emerged in 1954, and became the first and one of the most famous Tokusatsukaiju (monsters). Along with many techniques specifically formulated for it, *Godzilla* changed the landscape of Japanese science fiction and cinema, and created a uniquely Japanese vision of special-effects cinema. Today, while Hollywood film companies are making full use of digital tools to produce sophisticated and realistic screen monsters, the humble kaiju in Tokusatsu films still enjoy a certain market niche in Japan, and fans include both the old and the young. This could be due to the comparably lesser capitalisation of the Japanese film industry. They need to supply a good amount of fantasies set in a Japanese context to meet the audience's appetite, and thus the imaginative yet comparably roughly made Tokusatsu monsters could keep growing. It becomes a divergent Japanese vision of computer animation.

Character Animation (Pseudo-human Being)

The third process is the "pseudo-human being", such as goblins, aliens and mutants, that may resemble variants of human beings, but are not intended to simulate humans. They would be the best subjects with which to test the capacities of digital tools. In 1999 *The Mummy* shocked audiences with its convincing digital pseudo-human characters. Through a combination of motion capture, live action and computer, the menacing, "undead" high priest character of Imhotep was generated, with astonishingly detailed layers of muscles, sinew and tissue. Since then, digital visual effects artists have been busy turning live actors into photorealistic fantasy characters by using motion-capture technology. Completely CGI-generated, fully-articulated humanoid characters include Jar Jar Binks (in *Star Wars Episode I: Phantom Menace*, 1999), Gollum (in *The Lord of the Rings Trilogy*, 2001-2003), and the Hulk (in *Hulk*, 2003).

Worth noting here is that while Gollum, a photorealistic fantasy figure in motion-capture, has become one of the most acclaimed CGI characters in animation history, cartoon-like figures animated in motion-capture technique (like Jar Jar Binks and 2003's Hulk) have usually received negative reviews (Clinton 2003; Edelstein 1999; Harrison 1999; Staple 1999). Although these non-realistic characters seemed less popular with mainstream audience, they were intentionally designed to be non-realistic: George Lucas designed Jar Jar Binks in this way probably because he thought it could appeal to small children (Harrison 1999); Ang Lee chose an unsophisticated appearance for his Hulk to retain the feeling in the original comic books. However, the decisions to make these characters aiming at something depart from the canons of "realism" and "invisibility" would likely alienate audience. Besides, the Hulk is a mutated humanoid monster transformed directly from the human. The link between the live-action protagonist and the cartoony CGI creation may make it harder to accept the Hulk as a convincing creature. Comparisons between Ang Lee's Hulk and Louis Leterrier's more realist approach (*The Incredible Hulk* 2008) have become a topic of discussion among moviegoers. However, these debates are nothing when compared with those encountered by the last process – the manufacture of a human being.

Character Animation (Human Being)

To simulate a human being – a creature that, even though we may be unaware of it, we instinctively read in all its subtlety and nuance – and to merge it seamlessly with live-action backgrounds is not only difficult but perhaps also unlikely to be realised successfully. Just as realistic robots would cause panic in our life, realistic CGI human characters on the screen could provoke controversy. In 2001 the *Square Co.* adapted its most popular computer game into the virtual film *Final Fantasy: The Spirits Within*, which was the first fully CGI feature-length film with all the human characters computer generated, introducing the first photorealistic CGI heroine Aki Ross. In fact, before the film's release there was already scepticism about the virtual human being. It turned out to be a box office failure and led to the dissolution of its production company *Square Pictures*. Although its failure is ascribed mainly to the poor storyline, the physical appearance of Aki Ross the CGI human character also received mixed reviews (Ebert 2003; Mitchell 2011). For several years the film was held up as an object lesson in failure that led animation designers to stay away from realistic CGI human characters.

The technology, which essentially turns live actors into computer-animated figures, was criticised for delivering a creepy "dead eye" effect. This critique rejoins the hypothesis of "the uncanny valley" conceived of by Japanese roboticist Masahiro Mori in 1970. Now informing the works of animators, filmmakers, and video game designers, Mori's hypothesis was originally introduced for the production of robots. It states that as a robot is made more humanlike in its appearance and motion, the emotional response from a human being to the robot will become increasingly positive and empathic, until a point is reached beyond which the response quickly becomes that of strong repulsion (Mori 1970). The uncanny valley hypothesis has been repeatedly cited to prove that a realistic three-dimensional computer human character is not feasible (Gallagher 2007; Hiltzik & Pham 2001; Wolchover 2011).

As a result, pseudo-human being became the best option with which to bring the capacities of the computer into full play and avoid negative reactions. Since Aki Ross, new efforts to produce CGI humans have been seen in films like *The Polar Express* (2004), *Beowulf* (2007), *Christmas*

Carol (2009) and *The Adventures of Tintin: Secret of the Unicorn* (2011). On this latest effort, *New York Magazine* comments, "Tintin looks simultaneously too human and not human at all, his face weirdly fetal, his eyes glassy and vacant instead of bursting with animated life" (Buchanan 2011); a view shared by many critics (Brooks 2011; Dargis 2011; Rose 2011). It seems to re-confirm that creating a realistic CGI human is still a thankless task. However, these weirdly realistic computer human beings, as a product integrating machine vision (motion capture technology) and the animator's hand, certainly have the capacity to provoke perceptual realism in special ways. This in fact is also true for all digital imaging technology, since it has the capacity to not only create undetectable simulations, but also to subvert them in sophisticated ways. This double-faced disposition in digital imaging technology will be discussed in the next section.

1.3 Double-faced Disposition in Digital Imaging Technology

It is often stated that the formal attributes favoured in the evolution of techniques for digital imaging include simulation, photorealism, fluidity and seamless digital montage, among others (Manovich 2001; Darley 2000). Yet these attributes may all embrace something which is not as simple as it appears. Take the case of simulation. It is often considered that complete simulation – the ability to reproduce our real-world sense impressions so completely as to fool us into thinking that we are witnessing raw reality – is the implicit destination of digital media (Messaris & Humphreys 2006: xvi). Complete simulation seems to have been achieved fairly well by cinema; but what CGI simulates is not the real world, but the world seen by the camera lens. Therefore a term has been coined to describe the realism of computer-generated imagery: *photorealism*, which Manovich (2001: 200) describes as "the ability to fake not our perceptual and bodily experience of reality but only its photographic image".

Audiences will see a great deal of lens-simulating effects such as out of focus, flare, wide-angle distortion, infrared night vision and the hand-held shaking effect which has been popular in computer animation (e.g. *Monster House*, 2006; *Surf Up*, 2007, *WALL-E*, 2009) in recent years. Additional efforts have been made to develop software and add-ons that could improve those lens-based effects (e.g. "Wheels" – the *Sony Imageworks* virtual camera system). Therefore, as Manovich (2001: 200) considers, the issue of the extraordinary capacity of digital tools to create realistic imagery is not about "what is real". The reason that some people think digital imaging technology has succeeded in faking reality is because that "cinema, over the course of the last hundred years, has taught us to accept its particular representational form as reality" (Manovich 2001: 200). Lister, et al. (2008: 138) also point out that, "photography here functions not as some kind of mechanically neutral verisimilitude but as a mode of representation that creates a 'reality effect'".

The use of digital imaging technology often presents a double-faced disposition. With their implications still relevant today, Manovich (2001) and Darley (2000) have both pointed out that, while being technologically advanced, digital imaging technology actually recovers some of the aesthetic features dominant in pre-cinematic forms. This can be seen as a comment on the double-faced disposition of digital imaging technology. A more direct framing may come from *Remediation: Understanding New Media*. In this book, Bolter & Grusin (1999) examine the mutually constructive strategies showed by digital technologies, and introduce two concepts useful in understanding the digital technologies explored in their pages: immediacy and hypermediacy.

Hypermediacy is defined as a "style of visual presentation whose goal is to remind the viewer of the medium", while immediacy is a "style of visual presentation whose goal is to make the viewer forget the presence of the medium (canvas, photographic film, cinema, …) and believe that he/she is in the presence of the objects of representation" (Bolter &Grusin 1999: 272-73). The constituent elements of the two can work together and reinforce each other. Similarly, there is a double-faced disposition in digital imaging technology: one dimension relates to creating perfect perceptual realism, and the other relates to disturbing perceptual realism in its unique ways. To provide further illustration of this argument, in the following paragraphs I will look at three particular capacities of digital imaging technology – texture mapping, seamless compositing, and realistic human characters. In the previous section on "character animation (human being)", the challenge of creating a realistic human being has been delineated; the following section on "realistic human characters" suggests its potential to turn the uncanniness into an advantage for artists to exploit.

Texture Mapping

Texture mapping can be taken as an example of the double-faced quality. It is a method for adding detail, surface texture or colour to a computer-generated model. It is now a technique so common that we may have become unaware of its significance. As Heckbert (1986: 1) points out, in the early days of digital technologies, in the quest for more realistic imagery, "one of the most frequent criticisms of early 3-D computer generated images was the extreme smoothness of surfaces, as they showed no texture, bumps, scratches, dirt, or finger-prints". The application of texture mapping to 3-D graphics can efficiently fix this. Pioneered by Edwin Catmull in his Ph.D. thesis of 1974, texture mapping is now extensively used and is one of the primary techniques to improve the appearance of objects.

Through the application of texture mapping, a simple polygon can appear to be made of wood or stone or any other materials, depending on the pattern on the two-dimensional texture. This technique is neither the replication of world through camera, nor the representation of world through the artist's hand; it is rather a blending of photography and painting through algorithms. Usually the texture itself is a mixture of photograph and hand-painting. Enhanced by the artist's hand, the photorealistic texture on the three dimensional object seems to create something beyond realism. It seems to have the ability to make the stone stony and un-stony at the same time.

It is interesting to look at the effect when we replace most of the sets and props in a live-action film with CGI. It is now possible for a director to shoot an entire film in front of a blank background (often a green screen) and then merge it with computer-generated environment during post-production. Films such as *Sky Captain and the World of Tomorrow* (2004), *Sin City* (2005), *300* (2007), *Speed Racer* (2008) and *Alice in Wonderland* (2010) use this kind of digital background environment entirely or for most of the scenes. It is often used to show something impossible or too expensive to build as a real set. Sometimes it is used for specific aesthetic effects. For example, many of the scenes in *Sin City*, such as the hotel room, the bar and the road, are not impossible or too expensive to be produced by hand-built sets, but the film is still shot almost entirely in front of a green screen. The extensive use of a virtual environment is actually an attempt to create the look and feel of the action comic book world through a combination of live action and graphics. Although the virtual settings are "realistic", replacing the real objects with digitisation does create a feeling of the unreal. The result, as some film critics have complained, is that the city "feels uninhabited", in which "the social anxiety and psychological unease of the old film noirs has been digitally broomed away" (Scott 2005); the digitisation plays a part in making it "hard to get pulled into the story on any level other than the visceral" (Dargis 2005). However, the sense of the non-human and unreal is perhaps exactly what the director aspires to.

The double-faced disposition is also explored in the practice of this study. In the middle part of *Flying Tunes*, when the two actors stand apart on their balconies and play opposite each other, the backgrounds, including buildings and balconies are all virtual, made by 3-D computer software. Thanks to the texture (adapted from photos of real buildings) and lighting, these buildings neither present much of the possible rigidity of primary CGI nor appear to be real buildings. They look more like models or enlarged miniatures. The effect makes the whole background stage-like, and may go a step further to estrange the situation of the two actors. This aspect will be discussed in Chapter 3.

Digital Compositing

Digital compositing is another example showing how an implement devised for realism simultaneously possesses the potential to create a sense of alienation. Digital compositing is widely used within television, advertising, computer game, video and cinema production, and most other moving images in computer culture. It has now become a norm for creating moving imagery (Manovich 2001: 138). In the field of new media, the term "digital compositing" refers to the process of "combining a number of moving image sequences, and possibly stills, into a single sequence with the help of special compositing software" (Manovich 2001: 136-7). Both Manovich (2001) and Darley (2000) discuss its aesthetics– layered, intense and seamless – at length.

Manovich (2001: 155) emphasises that what is important is what happens on the edges where different images are joined. According to him, "the borders where different realities come together is the new arena where illusionist artists of our era try to outdo one another". Whether it is composing a live action video with 3-D computer generated material or composing various photographic or cinematographic elements together, the main problem is no longer how to generate convincingly looking individual images but how to blend them together. Darley (2000: 115) considers that the mimetic accuracy and the seamless character of computer synthesised imagery is in keeping with the illusionist aesthetic generally predominant within contemporary Hollywood. While doing so, the bizarre nature of the imagery similarly denies and simultaneously points to the highly sophisticated artifice involved in its production. "It is both the bizarre and impossible nature of that which is represented and its thoroughly analogical character (simulation of the photographic), that fascinates, produces in the viewer a 'double-take' and makes him or her want to see it again, both to wonder at its portrayal and to wonder about 'just how it was done'" (ibid.). As a result, although it is mostly used to increase the feel of realism of composited footage, it might work as a tool to stimulate audiences' awareness of the image as well.

The most challenging aspect of digital compositing may occur in the production of hybridised characters – the partly cinematographic, partly computer-generated figure. To a large extent, the aim of the compositing technique is to create audience involvement. Take Captain Davy Jones in

Pirate of the Caribbean: Dead Man's Chest (2006) as an example. The appearance of this fictional character is a mixture of various aquatic flora and fauna features. His most striking feature is the cephalopod-like head, with octopus-like tentacles giving the illusion of a thick beard. Throughout the film, Davy Jones uses the tentacles of his "beard" like fingers to manipulate objects. Produced on computer, this weird "beard" looks vivid and natural, and could not be achieved by traditional prosthetics. But because the effect is so realistic, some film reviewers mistakenly identified it as some kind of prosthetic makeup (Gilbey 2007). It nevertheless is successful in enabling the audience to be immersed in the story and forget the use of digital effects.

Sometimes the result can be intriguingly strange, arousing both a sense of unease and curiosity as to how it was produced. The mutated creature in *Slice* (2009), for example, is a character that may attract audience scrutiny. The scientist in the film splices together human and animal DNA to create a half-human, half-bird-like creature who she names Dren ("nerd" spelled backwards). As a toddler, Dren is a hairless, bird-like, lizard creature with monocular vision, each eye positioned on opposite sides of its head. As it grows up, the eyes gradually shift toward the front. The adult Dren becomes an "attractive" young female with bald head, the eyes slightly far apart and slanted. The film's writer-director Vincenzo Natali pointed out in an interview that the look of Dren is a subtractive design: "Our prime directive was to make a creature that we could believe really exists. And the way to do that, I felt, was to be subtractive. Most movie monsters are additive. What I wanted to do with Dren, in her later stages, was to change the human form in subtle ways. I felt the small changes would actually be more shocking than the big ones. If you make a small change to somebody's face, it is much more jarring than some kind of gross deformation" (McCarthy 2010). Actually, the adult Dren's eyes were not computer generated. They used real footage of the actress's eyes which are moved and then projected back on her head. Everything is real, but subtly moved. The resulting appearance is different and appealing. For some reviewers the design of Dren is what makes the film special (Dargis 2010; Schwarzbaum 2010).

Madame Tutli-putli, the 2008 Best Short Film winner at Cannes, is an experimental animated film that uses an unusual and challenging technique in the way it depicts the model characters' eyes. Part of its excellence is its powerful visual blending of live action and stop frame animation. The production team's challenge at the beginning of the filmmaking process was to devise a method of giving the puppets some real soul (Seymour 2008). After considering various approaches they came upon the idea of tracking real human eyes on the faces of stop motion puppets. The resulted effect is compelling. The conflicting yet seamless combination of a lifeless silicone appearance and vivid real eyes brings a productive visual result for the character.

In the practice *Flying Tunes* there is also one scene that features the eyes. In the last part of the film, the fly starts to harass the two actors directly. Before the harassment their performance are captured by normal live-action shooting. When the harassment starts everything changes. In order to stop the fly, the girl shuts her face flat with a book. The fly then goes to the boy and flies around his head. Following the flying fly, the boy's eyes move in circles turning from the front to the back and then to the front again. These impossible behaviours are of course achieved by digital compositing. Following a series of non-digital-enhanced live-action performance in the previous scenes, the seamless compositing helps in bringing unexpectedness with these caricatures. On the one hand, digital compositing merges the boundaries between mundane and ridiculous; on the other hand, it actually underlies the distinctions between them.

Realistic Human Characters

The production of realistic human character may also be considered as another aspect of the double-faced disposition of digital imaging technology. Some designers and researchers believe in the promise that one day the simulated human being will become so indistinguishable from the flesh-and-blood co-stars that they can perform together without being recognised as a special effect (e.g. North 2008: 3). However, to realise this belief is very difficult.

Hollywood director Robert Zemeckis's attempts to create completely computer-generated photorealistic cinema by utilising motion-capture technology can be taken as an example. While moviegoers considered this kind of filmmaking to be a novelty, they did not really think it was successful as can be seen in constant criticisms such as "I don't see the point of performance capture";"they have neither the spark of true life nor that of an artist's unfettered imagination"; and "it's more about muscular technology than art" (Reader's comment about the review of *Beowulf* movie cited by Dargis 2009). As shown in previous section on "character animation (human being)", the uncanny valley is often seen as a measure of audience response to these CGI films. The idiomatic expression of "uncanny" is often translated as scary or creepy, and the "valley"as the drop in positive human reaction when measured on a graph. Obviously the "synthespians" (North 2008: 2) in Zemeckis's films have not crossed Mori's uncanny valley yet. Yet, is it possible to utilise the "creepy eyes" and make them something positive and useful for the storyline?

Rise of the Planet of the Apes (2011) used a great deal of motion capture animation. The chimpanzees, gorillas and orang-utans that star in the film are all computer generated. As with human characters, this representation of humankind's closest relatives also proved problematic in terms of fooling the human eye. Our human eyes are finely tuned to detect problems with those depictions, and the illusion can be easily broken. But the CGI creatures in *Rise of the Planet of the Apes* were generally praised as realistic, even by a primatologist (Eisenberg 2011). Audience response to *Rise of the Planet of the Apes* was quite positive. The apes seem to be free from the death tinge of the uncanny valley. This raises the issue of whether they have crossed the uncanny valley and why the realistic CGI creature in this film does not alienate the audience. The motion capture animation in it is phenomenal, yet the audience can certainly tell the difference between real filmed footage and computer animation; the apes are not so realistic that they have crossed the uncanny valley. However, Cangialosi (2011) suggests that the uncanny valley in this case helps the story by visually supporting a duality in its premise: "As a moviegoer, we are sympathizers to Caesar's plight and subsequent primate revolution; thus we root for the apes. On the other side of the brain, as humans we are freaked out by the possibility that apes could overthrow the simian order." Moreover, as we know that Caesar the ape is performed by Andy Serkis via motion capture effects, "knowing there is a man behind the mask, digital or latex, we are reassured" (ibid.).

Nevertheless, apes are not humans, no matter how closely they are related to humans. Realistic CGI humans are still very difficult to win acceptance from our hyper-picky brains. The realistic characters in *The Adventures of Tintin: The Secret of the Unicorn* (2011) are an example. Directed by Steven Spielberg and Peter Jackson, this film was well constructed in terms of its storylines, pacing, and characters and received generally positive reviews. But it has also been criticised as having uncanny valley issues. Brooks (2011) in *The Guardian* comments: "While the big set pieces are often exuberantly handled, the human details are sorely wanting. How curious that Hergé achieved more expression with his use of ink-spot eyes and humble line drawings than a bank of computers and an army of animators were able to achieve. On this evidence, the film's pioneering 'performance capture' techniques is still too crude and unrefined. In capturing the butterfly, it kills it too."

He goes on to describe the experience of watching the CGI humans in *Tintin* as "partying with ghosts". Reading this, I cannot help but wonder whether it might be possible to have a story featuring characters that are "beautiful but dead", and it might indeed be enjoyable for the audience to "party with ghosts". Maybe Tintin is simply a cherished comic book character that is not suitable for realistic motion capture animation. Robinson (2011) reckons that what makes Tintin universally beloved by readers of all ages is exactly what makes him a tricky lead character on screen.He says: “while a blank slate character is perfect for comic book adventures, allowing any reader to imagine him or herself in Tintin’s place, it makes for a rather ho-hum character [for a film].” Whether Tintin is a successful screen character or not, here I see that while digital imaging technology is used to create unprecedentedly realistic illusion, it also has the potential to create something different from realism.

What the digital provides can be two-sided, powerful in one respect but also the inverse. The repulsion aroused by the appearance and motion between a “barely-human” and “fully-human” entity could be utilised to induce a subtle alienation or to create tension between plausibility and the uncanny. Since CG realistic human figure easily falls into an uncanny situation, could this be an advantage for the artist to seize?

In this study motion capture is not the subject of the experiment in the practice. For an independent filmmaker, motion capture animation is an unlikely option given the amount – and expense – of the technical resources required. The result will very likely become simply crude rather than experimental. In this study I chose pixilation, the technique conceptually opposite to rotoscoping and motion capture, to be the centre of my technical experiments.

I wished to clarify the following questions:

1) With the help of digital imaging technology, can pixilation be endowed with a double-faced quality?
2) While the jiggly and discontinuous movement is of significance as mentioned in Section 1.1, can it be the opposite that generates specific meanings?
3) Although pixilated figures are already hybridised, can they be “further” hybridised with the help of the digital? These questions have formed the base of my interrogation of pixilation in the project. All these are explored in the practice and throughout the writings of following chapters.

I wished to highlight that, for moving images in the digital era, the double-faced quality in my view not only exists, but also requires, and would richly reward, more theoretical attention. While digital’s capacity for achieving the effects of realism attracts much mainstream cinema attention, the accompanying sense of the unreal, because of its special aesthetic function, is also worth noting. Before deciding that defective realism is a failure, it may be beneficial for an independent practitioner to take a different point of view, evaluating the performance in terms of how a double-faced quality is expressed, and how this functions in delivering messages.

To summarise, this chapter explains the opposing attributes of live action and animation. The discussion in Section 1.1suggests a dialectic relationship of negation or supplementation between live action and animation. From this relationship one can grasp the opposed tendencies embraced across the whole field of the moving image. The advent of digital technology has had a great impact on moving images, including new ways of challenging perceptual realism, exposing or employing the tension between the opposed tendencies. Some would argue that the most significant capacity of digital imaging technology lies in its ability to completely simulate an object, environment or figure. However, this could be taken inversely, as a capacity to alienate within the moving image as a medium. To discuss this, Section 1.2 first describes the special effects tradition inherited by computer-generated imagery, followed by an inspection of digital imaging technology's potential to induce tension between live action and animation in Section 1.3. While researches looking at digital imaging technology often focus on its ability to perfect illusion and the impact of this on filmic realism, my research is more concerned with its specific ability to "imperfect" the illusion, and more significantly, the implications for the practice of filmmaking.

CHAPTER TWO

FROM UNCANNY TO ESTRANGEMENT

As stated in Chapter 1, live action and animation can be seen as an opposing pair that enacts a dynamic relationship of negation or supplementation. It was also noted that while the relationship between them is often used to create harmonised perceptual realism, especially in mainstream cinema, my project is more concerned with interrupting perceptual realism in a meaningful way. This chapter further explains how such interruptions are created and make sense in the practice of this project. It explores and discusses concepts of the uncanny, defamiliarisation and estrangement, as well as suture theory and derealisation. My methods of exploiting supplementary materials and meanings are explained from three standpoints: the first is the significance of the experience of the supplementary to hybrid-film experimentation; the second considers how treating and understanding hybridised character from layers of consciousnesses can benefit a sense of aesthetic estrangement; and the last connects estrangement to the derealisation of hyperrealism.

2.1 Creating the Experience of the Supplementary

The integration of live action and animation, which are taken as mobile opposites in this thesis, partake in an integrated presence, and could be comprehended through the logic of supplementarity. The experience of supplementary is vital to the hybrid film. This can be grasped from two perspectives: firstly with regards to the concept of the uncanny. The theory of the uncanny has gained renewed significance in the last few decades (for example, Kristeva 1991; Castle 1995; Grenville 2002; Tie 2004; Ramey 2005; Johnson 1999; Weight 2006). It also has been a lively topic in debates on the aesthetics of hybrid film (Cholodenko 1991; Gunning 2008). In what follows I also suggest that the interface between live action and animation can be characterised by its uncanniness. Freud's seminal essay "The Uncanny" (*Das Unheimliche*) describes how the feeling of the uncanny may arise on many occasions, one of which is in the experience of the supplementary. As pointed out in Royle's *The Uncanny: An Introduction* (2003), the supplementary may happen in a situation when one person or figure becomes a substitute, a supplementary or substitutive role for another person or figure; or it may occur in a strange actuality of supplementary or prosthetic limbs. When considered in terms of its connection with the uncanny, the experience of the supplementary provides a profitable point of departure for an aesthetic investigation.

The second aspect concerns suture theory. Suture theory was first introduced by Jean-Pierre Oudart, and drew on Jacques Lacan's notion of subject formation and Jacques-Alain Miller's subsequent work on this topic. It has been further elaborated by film critics such as Daniel Dayan, Stephen Heath and Kaja Silverman, and has also been discussed by scholars such as David Bordwell and Noel Carroll. George Butte (2008: 287) suggests that the suture's narration of subjectivities could be framed by two of Maurice Merleau-Ponty's concepts. The first is from Merleau-Ponty's 1948 essay "The Film and the New Psychology" where the wholeness, simultaneity, and relatedness of human perceptions are stressed when he states, "the meaning of the shot depends on what precedes it in the movie, and the succession of scenes creates a new reality which is not merely the sum of its parts" (Merleau-Ponty 1964a [1948]: 54-55). The second is Merleau-Ponty's later notion of chiasmus. For example, in his 1964 essay "The Intertwining – The Chiasm" Merleau-Ponty (1968 [1964]: 143) provides an image: "There is a circle of the touched and the touching, the touched takes hold of the touching; there is a circle of the visible and the seeing, the seeing is not without visible existence". In the handshake, where each experiences being touched in touching, I "touch in it the same poser to espouse the things that I have touched in my own" (141). In this there is a transcending of difference as my movements "address themselves to the body in general and for itself" (143). As Merleau-Ponty (ibid.) explains, the circle that includes seeing others see oneself seeing "betray[s] the solipsist illusion … that every going beyond is a surpassing accomplished [only] by oneself". In other words, it is always an imperfectly joined web of experiences that makes subjects simultaneously present and absent to each other. Images from Merleau-Ponty's other essays also expresses this complexity. For example, in *Signs*: "There is said to be a wall between us, but it is a wall we build together, each putting a stone in the niche left by the other" (1964b [1960]: 19), or, in an earlier essay: "There is a woven between us an "exchange," a "chiasm between two destinies," in which there are never quite two of us, and yet one is never alone" (1970 [1953]: 82). The following example opens up the possibility of seeing chiasm as suture even more clearly:

"Chiasm …: the insertion of the world between the two leaves of my body/ the insertion of my body between the 2 leaves of each thing and of the world" (1968 [1964]: 264). Here, as Butte (2008: 18) argues, chiasm is a paradigm for embodied intersubjectivity, and suture as chiasm can be seen as an interleaving of embodiments. "In this understanding of the representation of consciousnesses in film, even cutting apart may be a deeply intersubjective narrative" (ibid.).

Of interest to my thesis is what Butte says about the suture of consciousnesses, and I will uses these ideas to explore how the experience of the supplementary can be used for the production of layers of consciousnesses. Through the suture of their consciousness, live-action and animated characters can become doppelgangers to each other. This offers them a self-reflexive relationship, and makes them a single entity while at the same time two individual figures. Through experience of the supplementary, therefore, the conceptual and physical aspects of the integration of live action and animation can become co-dependent.

Hybrid Film and the Uncanny

My consideration of the uncanny first emerged from the process of practice production. As mentioned in the Introduction, the first practice for this project, *Nothing to Do with Weather*, was developed around a concern to integrate the different characteristics of live action and animation, to create a site open to various meeting points between them. Although it was designed to respond to technical issues, I soon found that the attempt to keep my practice in a (technically) liminal state echoed the experience of my first year studying abroad, which was also a time and condition of transition. A theme was therefore developed around a feeling of alienation, not-belonging, which also thematically reflects the tension between live action and animation.

The state of being depicted in *Nothing to Do with Weather* reminded me of the uncanny as an uneasy but not entirely frightening psychological concept when talking about "a strangeness of framing and borders, an experience of liminality" (Royle 2003: 2). Without having deliberately designed to be so, the relationship between the drawn and photographic girls seems to correspond to the concept of the double, considered by Freud (2009 [1919]: 140-1) to be one of the most prominent themes of the uncanny. As mentioned in the Introduction, the uncanny may emerge, according to Freud, when a double reality is created and what was once familiar becomes unfamiliar; it can be the feeling of meeting your doppelganger. In *Nothing to Do with Weather*, the live-action character has an animated doppelganger. The retrospective review of the relationship between the live-action and animated characters further aroused my interest and consideration of the Freudian uncanny, and stimulated more attempts to approach the double in the other two works. For example, according to Freud (2009 [1919]: 141), the phenomenon of the double can be accentuated "by transferring mental processes from the one person to the other – what we should call telepathy – so that the one possesses knowledge, feelings and experience in common with the other". Therefore, in *Animating Animator the Animated,* the idea of the double is intended in the scene featuring telepathic connection, induced by the spider, between the animator and the animated. In *Flying Tunes* the relationship between the two actors, who are of different sexes, can also be a manifestation of the increasing correspondence of their actions that finally synchronise in the end. In these works the double can be seen as a way to explore the conflicts of personality or subjectivity.

The experience of being a foreigner, or feeling disoriented, are easy to relate to the uncanny, but early hybrid films also have a lot to do with the theme of uncanny strangeness where the uncanny often appears as magic, illusion, dismemberment and haunting events. One of the first special effects in the history of cinema, for example, is a reconstruction of decapitation in *The Execution of Mary Queen of Scot* (1895). In this very short film (which is only 18 seconds), although the actress is replaced by a mannequin before the executioner brings down the axe, the scene when the mannequin's head is chopped off and is held in the air can still horrify the audience. This kind of camera trick, the stop-action substitution technique, was believed to be first discovered and developed by French filmmaker George Melies, who pioneered the first double exposure (*La cavernemaudite*, 1898), the first split screen with performers acting opposite themselves (*Un Homme de tete*, 1898), and the first dissolve (*Cendrillon*, 1899). As a recurring theme in his work, the operation of head displacement is used extensively in *The Melomaniac* (1903), where the conductor improvises a stave comprising six notes by pulling off his head six times and throwing them onto the wires.

The aesthetic of early hybrid work parallels many of the qualities attributed to the uncanny. The world of object animation, in which an object is moved or reshaped by small increments between individually photographed frames, creating the illusion of movement when the series of frames are played as a continuous sequence, is abundant in the experimental hybrid films, and is also a means of expressing the uncanny. Object animation is already a combination of photography and frame-by-frame manipulation, no matter what objects are manipulated – a chair, a rock, a puppet or a piece of clay – to present the tension between live action and animation. Giving life or spirit to lifeless furniture, toys, puppets or dead insects could produce a kind of bewildering lifelikeness, and might be more frequently associated with the generic term "animation". Puppet animation especially continues and extends the tradition of puppet theatre in Eastern Europe, a tradition that has accumulated aesthetic resources such as: sophisticated carved marionettes; exquisitely sewn costumes with the craftsmanship emulating that of a wedding dress or mortuary garment; magic effects of smoke and light; invisible wires manipulated by a puppet master; automatic doors, secret passages and wheel axles behind a stage filled with automata – various gadgets operated by mechanical devices. This is a haunted world. The puppets, stage properties and gadgets – no matter how light or heavy they are – always maintain gravity. They inhabit a concrete and tangible space, with shadows concealing the space behind them. And those concealed corners/spaces, where the wandering soul crouches, are one of the origins of our deep fear of the unknown.

Russian-born Polish filmmaker LadislasStarevich (1892-1965) was a great pioneer of stop-motion animation and animated puppets to tell consistently coherent stories. He was famous for using insects or other animals as his protagonists. These creatures live in miniatures of buildings and streets, and in some cases have carefully scaled cars. The realistic and detailed miniature sets enhanced the uncanny aspects of these dramas. Examining *The Cameraman's Revenge*, which Crafton considered the best of Starevich's works (Crafton 1993:239), Telotte (2010: 39) illustrates how Starevich used a fully three-dimensional world for a larger strategy. Through the movement in depth, Starevich's strategy is to "take his audience into a normally unseen or hidden realm, hereby revealing not only its depths but also its similarities to our own world, and ultimately the normally unseen – or purposely hidden – dimensions of that world". In this way his animated films potently suggest another world at the same time parallel to and coexistent with our own, through which we are associated with the animated inhabitants of the films.

This kind of supplementary life raises the question of life in terms of our daily life's most mundane experience. Royle (2003: 23) points out that the uncanny is not merely an "aesthetic" or "psychological" matter, for its elaboration is necessarily bound up with "analysing, questioning and even transforming what is called 'everyday life'". This dimension is reflected by Czech surrealist animator Jan Svankmajer comment on animation:

> Animation enables me to give magical powers to things. In my films, I move many objects, real objects. Suddenly, everyday contact with things which people are used to acquire a new dimension and in this way casts a doubt over reality. In other words, I use animation as a means of subversion (Quoted in Wells 1998: 11).

Many of Svankmajer's works manifest the subversive ability of the uncanny strangeness induced by moving objects in mundane situations.

His *Picnic with Weismann* (1968), for example, sets the scene of a relaxing picnic where normal things like music, fruit and chess game are enjoyed by a man's clothes rather than the man. The man himself is tied up and imprisoned in the wardrobe, and finally he is buried alive by two shovels. The clothes, chess, photograph and the shovels all move automatically in this creepy world. To a rational person of the modern age, it appears to be ridiculous/primitive to think of everyday life as uncanny or imbued with magic. Interestingly, there are scholars who have noticed that the uncanny might be a distinctively modern experience (Collins & Jervis 2008). If we connect the emergence of automatic machines – such as cars, trains, washing machines or others – with furniture that moves automatically in object animation film, the appearance of modern life does not seem so far removed from a world governed by ghosts or spectres.

From an examination of James Stuart Blackton's *The Haunted Hotel* (1907) and contemporaneous hybrid films using stop-motion techniques, Crafton (1993: 32) comments on the earliest film animators, "Are these curious filmmakers playing with bringing their puppets and household objects to life far from Shelley's *Frankenstein* and similar homunculus themes in romantic literature?". Classifying these earliest filmmakers as ancestors of science fiction who were writing metaphorically of the scientific revolution, Crafton (1993: 32-3) summarises his observation:

> Perhaps the gothic and scientific subjects of early animation … are comprehensible as images of the turn-of-the-century fascination with self-propulsion. The automobile and the airplane were wonderful inventions because they represented totally liberating freedom of movement. These objects moving with what seemed their own internal life were reflected when the normally inanimate objects of everyday life – furniture, tools, toys, even pictures – lurched into sputtering motion on the screen. Unexpectedly, through the marvellous "electrical" invention of the cinematograph, the whole world appeared to be in flux, as though electricity and internal combustion were secrets of the universe. For the most part the animation sequences in these first films serve no narrative function; they exist only as movement for its own sake. Although some may view this as "primitive", it demonstrates that even at the beginning the makers of animated films were, like earlier romantics, fascinated with the materials of artistic creation. These subjects, then, however "haunted", were also representations of animators' enduring concern with autokinesis, movement in itself, the stuff of animation.

Referring to Crafton's commentary, Cholodenko (2007: 495) declares that the continued appeal of these filmmakers is the enduring fascination with bringing to life with motion, with the artificing of life, "an artificing that takes us back to classical times, to the artificial man of the automaton and to the "rival" traditions of animism and mechanism." Moreover, through theorising the filmic/cinematic apparatus as animatic apparatus, Cholodenko (2007: 496) points out that "the filmic apparatus is neither merely a machine, nor what it images merely mechanical, for it confounds, disseminates and seduces the very opposition of organic and mechanical, animism and mechanism". As a result, there are always liminal explorations in the filmmaking process, especially – as I would like to emphasise in this research – for live-action/animated hybrids practice.

As automation is central to modern technology, it could be said that the uncanny features in our modern life. "Magic", "disenchantment" and "rationalisation"…, all these can be reminiscent of the Enlightenment, a period in the history of Western thought and culture, stretching from the mid-seventeenth century through the eighteenth century, characterised by dramatic revolutions in science, philosophy, society and politics (Stanford Encyclopaedia of Philosophy 2010). Although often traced back to Freud, the history of the uncanny as a ghostly feeling and concept goes back to at least the Enlightenment. As stated by Crary (1992, 133), David Brewster, the inventor of the stereoscope, believed that "the maintenance of barbarism, tyranny, and popery had always been founded on closely guarded knowledge of optics and acoustics, the secrets by which priestly and higher castes ruled". Brewster thus optimistically saw the spread of scientific ideas in the nineteenth century undermining the possibility of phantasmagoric effects. Interestingly, "phantasmagoric" is a word that Adorno, Benjamin, and others have used to describe forms of representation after 1850 (Crary 1992: 132). The process of modernity has been considered as closely connected to the emergence of a specific dimension of the uncanny. As Mladen Dolar (1991: 7) has pointed out, in pre-modern societies "the dimension of the uncanny was largely covered (and veiled) by the area of the sacred and untouchable", which was "assigned to a religiously and socially sanctioned place"; however, "with the triumph of the Enlightenment, this privileged and excluded place was no more". As a result, the age of reason or the Enlightenment produced "a new human experience of strangeness, anxiety, bafflement, and intellectual impasse" (Castle 1997: 8). Adorno believed that art is the disenchantment of the world (Adorno 1984: 80); and, as mentioned in the Introduction, literary critic Harold Bloom believes that canonical works have to do with "strangeness" (Bloom 1994: 2). These two attitudes may seem unrelated, but actually they overlap, since Adorno was taking the methodology of art as part of modernity, while Bloom saw the creative process as producing the effect of the uncanny. These two attitudes therefore both attribute to art the feature of anxiety, especially the anxiety cause by rationalisation. The concept of the uncanny enables reflection on formal and thematic issues for the integration of live action and animation. It may also endow the practice with an understanding of the modern conditions characterised by the digital. The experience of supplementary, as a possible trigger and one of the features of the uncanny, is for this reason emphasised in this project.

Rather than using objects or puppets, all three films utilise stop motion to animate human beings. On the one hand they are "alive" people who have relinquished their initiative of action. On the other hand they are required to exert extreme control and self-awareness in order to master their occasional involuntary body or facial actions during the long hours of shooting, i.e. trembling from fatigue. The puppet-like human being, I believe, could produce the kind of bewildering lifelikeness of puppet animation as described above. Moreover, the overlaying of live/dead, active/passive and resistance/obedient could address issues of being alive in a more subtle way. The opposing qualities coexist within a pixilated figure, suspending it in indeterminacy and ambiguity, a supplement of itself, and an experience of supplementary.

Layers of Consciousnesses and the Suture

In further considering the coexistence of opposing qualities within the subject and its possible effect we shall start the inquiry by looking at rotoscoping – an animation technique that is conceptually the reverse of pixilation but in some way very similar to it – because of its popularity in both mainstream and experimental films as well as in discussions among scholars.

Rotoscoping is a technique that allows animators to trace filmed footage of human movement into drawn sequences, frame by frame. It was invented by American filmmaker Max Fleischer (1883-1972). To test out this new invention, Max Fleischer photographed his brother Dave in a clown costume. After tracing the film, a process that involved a year's work producing 2,500 drawings, in 1919 the first rotoscoped character, Koko the Clown, was born, in the "Out of the Inkwell" series in which he featured. The rotoscoped Koko knew that he was made of ink. As Telotte (2010: 83) suggests, his moves to get out of the inkwell and get rid of the cartoonist reflect his efforts to escape his lifeblood, from the conventional space of animation to the real world, and to escape his established social role.

Rotoscoping also offered a tool with which to play with the films' artificial nature. Telotte (2010: 174) argues that the naturalised motion and seamless suture of different image sources (e.g. drawn figures and filmic space) had actually been beneficial in producing a high degree of reflexiveness and surreal results. Crafton (1993: 174) argues that the great attraction of these cartoons "was not so much the elaboration of the 'out of the inkwell' formula [of their 'KoKo the Clown' films] as the magical sense of realistic movement made possible by therotoscope". This effect was described in contemporaneous reviews which, as Ward (2004: 36) indicates, focus on the "marvel" or "magic" of the movement. In fact, while designed to produce a more "lifelike" or naturalistic motion, and to seamlessly combine animated motion with live action, the effect rotoscoping confers is an uncanny simulation of life and motion, human and nonhuman. Commentators rarely fail to identify an uncanny, jarring quality to rotoscoped animation. Examining a Fleischer Studio cartoon from 1932 called *Betty Boop's Bamboo Isle*, Bouldin (2001: 50) describes how the rotoscoped body stands out, the "realism" of its form and motion undermining itself, making the rotoscoped body seem unreal and unbelievable within the plastic physics of an animated universe. In the rotoscoped dance scene in *Bamboo Isle*, Betty's body seems strangely possessed; she moves differently and seems to hold herself differently from films in which she is totally drawn, i.e. without reference to live-action. Whether it is intended or not, the eerie effect brought about by the use of rotoscoping imparts an intriguing sense of existence to the character. The audience cannot at first sight correctly categorise/comprehend its movement and performance, as well as its lifelikeness. This may have affected the acceptance of rotoscoping as a cartoon technique. When this technique first appeared, few people queried whether rotoscoping could or should be considered animation/cartooning. However, with the maturity of character animation in the 1930s, and then the animated feature film, cartoon's mainstream became clear. The idea of a "real" cartoon became relatively fixed. The technique of rotoscoping was no longer automatically taken as synonymous with animation/cartoon.

At any rate the influence of this live-action tracing animation technique is significant. Even the most advanced motion-capture technique developed in the digital age shares a very similar concept with it. However, the position of the rotoscope in histories of animation is a contested one. On the one hand, rotoscoping was considered as a problematic animation technique for it often causes an incoherence of style: as long as it was designed to increase realist representation, it seems not to belong to the "cartoonal" world (Surman 2003/2004). On the other hand, the manifestation of rotoscope or the intermingling of animation and live-action can be effective in producing layered meaning and a "spectrality" or "thickening" to the overlaying of the presence of the real human performer and the animated representation (Bouldin 2003). Those are different layers/aspects of the same being, and dialogues occur between the layers/aspects. There have been several film theories about putting different filmic pieces together and explaining the dialogues between them. Here I would specifically consider the suture theory for its discussion of the establishment of subjectivity, which makes it especially pertinent in considering the experiencing of the supplementary.

In Merleau-Ponty's writings, chiasm is an image for the interweaving between the partially reversible perceptions of two (or more) consciousnesses; in which chiasm is "realized on the spot, by encroachment, thickness, *spatiality*" (Merleau-Ponty 1968: 264). The image of "a circle of the touched and the touching" (Merleau-Ponty 1968: 143), as Butte (2008: 293) explains,

> …expresses quite precisely Merleau-Ponty's sense of consciousnesses, of intersubjectivity, in the world; the thickness and spatiality of crisscrossing threads anchor each self in its body but also touch the other body, whose gestures mirror back one's gestures to oneself in a chain of intercorporeal responses that cannot be entirely hypothetical, entirely a delusion.

In this sense no individual possesses a pure, solipsistic self. The self is a relationship, a dynamic presence formed by the interaction, correlation or even mutual exclusion between individuals/subjects. It is the formation of consciousnesses. Every other subject or surrounding being that is consciously or unconsciously exchanging information/attitude/sensation with the individual is contributing to the layering of consciousnesses of the individual subject. Similarly, the arrangement of shots, camera angles and the editing of film sequences can function in suturing the layers.

The notion of building and suturing layers of consciousnesses is useful in approaching the supplementary. This is tested in the practice by establishing reciprocity between characters. For example, in *Flying Tunes* (fig. 2-1), through the process of gaze exchanging in the balcony scene, the intersubjectivity between characters is facilitated. With the gaze exchange between the lady in Victorian costume, who might be the substitute for the filmmaker, and the viewer, the interrelationship between the creator and the viewer is made possible. The two girls (graphic and photographic) in *Nothing to Do with Weather* (fig. 2-2) also have this kind of reciprocity. Their consciousnesses are layered through their giving and accepting of the book and cup. The graphic girl experiences the journey as a substitute or supplement for the photographic girl. And their supplementary relationship is enhanced and confirmed by the suture of their subjectivities. The suture generally happens between two subjects. Yet it can also be taken as happening within a singular subject if we see the two girls as the two corporalities of one subject. In this understanding of the representation of consciousnesses, even the integration of live action and animation within a character may be an intersubjective narrative, for it enables the narration of both internal conflict and compromise within the self-hood, especially when the hybridised figure exhibits disparate or heterogeneous characteristics that call for being sutured. This relates to my thinking about the use of hybridised figure made by rotoscoping or pixilation. In the previous discussion of the uncanny, due to its indeterminacy and ambiguity, the pixilated figure can be seen as a supplement of itself; while here it is recognised as already being in itself an embodiment of layered consciousnesses. In both cases the pixilated figure can be understood through experience of the supplementary. Bearing this in mind, the technique of pixilation is used deliberately in this project, aiming at the effects of estrangement and derealisation.

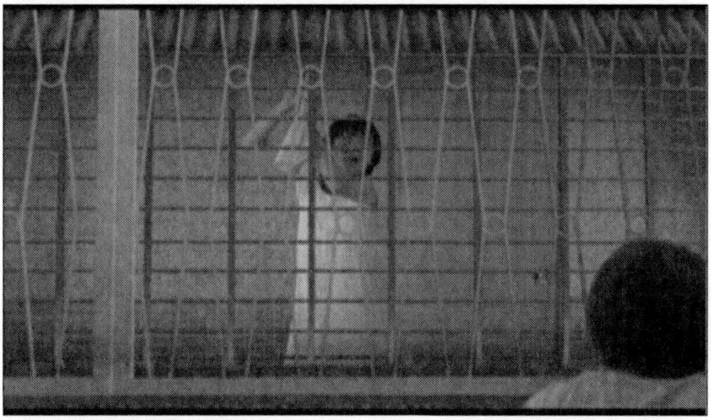

Fig. 2-1: Gaze exchanging in the balcony scene. Still from Flying Tunes

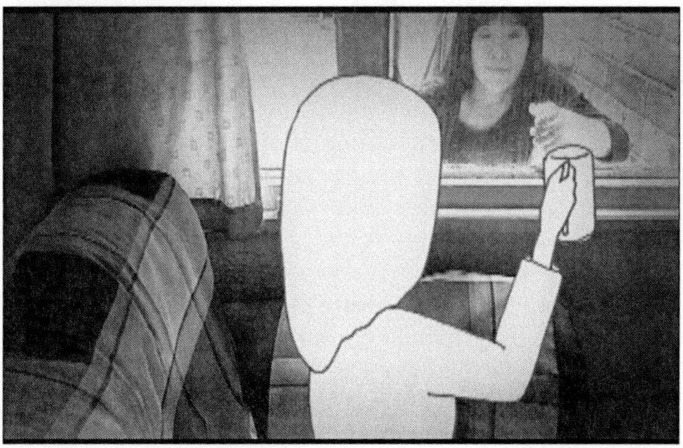

Fig. 2-2: Giving and accepting the cup between the drawn and photographic characters. Still from Nothing to Do with Weather.

2.2 Effect of Estrangement

In the world of experimental animation, due to its sometimes subversive and adventurous nature, there is no shortage of attempts to juxtapose diverse representation styles to disturb perceptual realism. For example, Estonian animation director Priit Parn's *The Triangle* (1982), a story about a love triangle between a married couple and a little man who lives under their stove, combines photo collages cut from glossy Western magazines to illustrate the way the husband and wife try on different faces to perpetuate each other's interest in their relationship. This technique, along with the unstable appearances of the characters (they seldom look the same from moment to moment), leads to a sense of shifting identity for each side of the triangle. *Everything Will be OK* (Don Hertzfeldt 2006), a collage of line drawings and photography, represents another kind of juxtaposition. The storyline follows a stick figure named Bill through his medical treatments and madness. By using experimental framing techniques, this film blends Hertzfeldt's classical minimal line-drawn style with fuzzy and fragmented real-world photography to express Bill's disorientation. A feeling of estrangement is well conveyed through his innovative technique in overlapping layers of consciousnesses through the operation of image and audio.

In this section I consider how treating and understanding hybridised character from layers of consciousnesses can enhance the sense of aesthetic estrangement. As a central concept of twentieth century art, "making it strange" is an artistic technique with which the Western intellectual world is familiar. Being a formalist approach, it has been extensively discussed and applied in art forms including literature, painting, music and dance. In the territory of film theory, although formalism is a minority view compared with that of the interpretive tradition, there have been detailed and strongly-argued studies developing a film formalist approach (Bordwell & Thompson 2006; Thompson 1981, 1988, 2009). As for animation theory, although formalist considerations regarding shape, colour and their transformation are essential to understanding an animated film, there has been less discussion of the concept of "making it strange". First coined and introduced in Russian critic Victor Shklovsky's famous essay "Art as Device" (1917), *ostranie* – often translated in English as "defamiliarisation" or "making it strange" – was considered as a way of understanding literary poetics. The Russian formalist notion was that the function of art is to renew and sharpen perception by breaking down our "automatised" recognition, and that this can be achieved by making the materials of art strange and more difficult to apprehend. In the frequently cited paragraph below Shklosky (1965: 11) accounts for this function concisely:

> Habitualisation devours works, clothes, furniture, one's wife, and the fear of war....Art exists that one may recover the sensation of life, it exists to make one feel things, to make the stone stony. The purpose of art is to impart the sensation of things as they are perceived and not as they are

> known. The technique of art is to make objects "unfamiliar", to make forms difficult, to increase the difficulty and length of perception because the process of perception is an aesthetic end in itself and must be prolonged.

The core idea of the technique of "making it strange" lies in avoiding habitualised expression, familiarised representation and cliché. It is inevitably affected by when, where, and by whom the art work is viewed. Obviously the effect of defamiliarisation is highly context dependent; the context may range from the larger scale, such as ethnicity and nationality, to very small, intimate and personal feelings. To explore this point, I would like to describe a personal experience to show how variable it can be.

The town of Loughborough is the first place where I experienced living in a Western country. I found that the colour purple is used a great deal in Loughborough. The brand colour of Loughborough University is purple: purple logo, purple T-shirt, purple badge, purple paint on the building and so forth. I assumed that the colour purple represents something good in Western culture. Otherwise it would not be used extensively and symbolically. After some research, I learned that in Europe purple is associated with nobility and spirituality; it is usually a signifier of wealth and status. As early as 400 BC, Plato (circa 429 – 347 B.C.) had delivered an encomium to the colour purple as below:

> Suppose that we were painting a statue, and some one came up to us and said, Why do you not put the most beautiful colors on the most beautiful parts of the body – the eyes ought to be purple, but you have made them black (Plato, Book IV, *The Republic*).

This "most beautiful" colour also stood for the "most obviously prized hue … in Antiquity" (Gage 1993: 16) and the "most enduring status symbol of the ancient world" (Reinhold 1970: 71). Later, with the Roman court's employment of legal mechanisms in their efforts to connect Tyrian purple with imperial power, the colour purple gradually became the symbol of royalty, power and the elite. The Emperors of the Holy Roman Empire, such as Marcus Aurelius, were "elevated to the purple". The Queen of Great Britain wears purple robes to signify her status. However the purple drew my attention before I read about its history. I was so attracted to it but at the beginning I did not know exactly why. The feeling it aroused is a bit weird but also intriguing. Then I remembered something twenty years ago. When I was an undergraduate student, one of our teachers was a dignified and conservative old professor. One day my best friend came to class wearing a purple jacket (a purple jacket was rare and so my friend loved it very much). He saw it and scolded my friend for wearing such a perverse colour. In Taiwan we all learned Confucius's *Analects* (c.a. 475 – 221 B.C.) in school; we knew the words of Confucius: "I hate purple that usurps red." (惡紫之亂朱) Confucius denounces purple because it is a mixed colour that results from the adulteration of the "pure" and "upright" colour of red. Confucius uses red as a metaphor for the virtue of simplicity that he regards as morally good. Purple, as a metaphor for multiplicity or duplicity, is morally bad and undesirable (Cai 1999: 333). This is why "to rob the red by the purple" (以紫奪朱) refers to acts of treachery or deceitfulness in ancient Chinese prose. Yet though we all learned Confucius's instructions, we seldom took them seriously, since they seemed quite irrelevant and distanced from our real life. We were startled by the professor's attitude to purple. But because of his reaction, I looked around our environment and noticed that purple was indeed not a popular colour in Taipei (at least twenty years ago). From then on I realised we were to some extent living in accordance with Confucian guidance while we thought we were very much Westernised in a modern city like Taipei. As time passed, this thought about purple, along with this small incident, passed into my unconsciousness and was forgotten. Twenty years later, the confrontation of the extensive use of purple at Loughborough awoke the memory and brought it back to my consciousness.

Purple became an intriguing colour for me. It stood out among all the colours, posing and waving, having a strange effect on me. To feel that feeling more, I bought purple clothes, purple stationery, and two purple umbrellas. I loved to use them and bring them out for they had such a strong sense of being. The small conflict between layers of consciousnesses exerted a special sensory effect on me. The co-existence of the two different understandings of purple estranged its meaning for me and foregrounded the colour whenever I met it. Walking around the campus looking at passing students, I wondered if there are people who, for some reasons, are also intrigued by this campus purple, a colour so prevalent that it might have become invisible to the students. This incident simply underlines two things: first, the encountering of overlaying of diverse consciousnesses can bring about the effect of estrangement; and second, the effect is richly varied and can be highly individualised. To further explain how context-dependent the audience's response could be, below I draw on the story related to my own culture, the story of China's first cartoon film.

In China, the first live-action/animated hybrid film, which is also the most commonly acknowledged as "China's first animated film", is *Da NaoHua Shi* (meaning "tumult in the studio" in Chinese) (1927) by the four Wan brothers (Laming and Guchan Wan, twin brothers born in 1900, and their younger brothers Chaochen and Dihuan Wan). It is reported that in the film a live-action artist (performed by Laming Wan) draws a little man who comes to life, leaves the drawing board, and causes havoc in the studio until the artist captures him and pins him to the drawing board (Zhu & Rosen 2010: 113). Apparently its story was very much influenced by the Fleischer brother's "Out of the Inkwell" series. Although has been praised in China's textbooks as a legendary beginning to China's animation history, it is unfortunately now lost, due to decades of extremely turbulent wartime (from the late nineteenth century to the early twentieth century). There were no contemporaneous written documents describing the film. According to Laming Wan's memoir, recorded in his later years, the making process was extremely difficult. Lacking technical knowledge and equipment, the Wan brothers produced this animated film with the measure of imitation by any alternative method they could think up (Zhu & Rosen 2010: 112-3). Yet the memoir mentioned nothing about using or trying to explore the use of rotoscoping – the lifelike animation style that composed the most notable aspect of the original Inkwell series. And the success of the film recorded in oral history or later presented in textbooks did not refer to rotoscoping either. It means that not only the Wan brothers but also the audience were not aware of its significance and unique aesthetic effect. Here, again, I want to emphasise that context is very crucial to the audience's appreciation of a work. Put in a different context, a copy of the Inkwell series, even without rotoscoping, could become a novelty.

In the discussion of the history of illusionism, Manovich connects cinema's "fake realities" with the cheery facades of Potemkin's villages, which convinced Catherine the Great that all Russian peasants were living in happiness and prosperity. Being a Russian-born scholar, Manovich does not hesitate to use metaphors from Russian culture to delineate his ideas. When considering an idea, I usually think about metaphors from Chinese culture (which seems to be inevitable). Here I would like to introduce a story told by Chinese philosopher Chuang-tzu (or Zhuangzi) (399 – 295 B.C.):

> Once upon a time, I, Zhuangzi, dreamed I was a butterfly, fluttering hither and thither, to all intents and purposes a butterfly. I was conscious only of following my fancies as a butterfly, and was unconscious of my individuality as a man. Suddenly, I awaked, and there I lay, myself again. Now I do not know whether I was then Zhuangzi dreaming I was a butterfly, or whether a butterfly is now dreaming it is me. Between Zhuangzi and a butterfly there is necessarily a barrier. This is called transformation of things (translated by Han 2009).

Chuang-tzu is an influential thinker in Taoist philosophy. One of his continuing interests was the issue of the interchangibility of appearance and reality. In this story he points out that a dream can seem as real as our waking existence. All the sights and sounds and feelings in the dream can be just as real and intense as our experience in reality. One of the key messages in this story is that if we can see how dreams can seem completely real, than we can see how reality can be just like a dream, and therefore we might gain detachment from emotional and material obsessions in our life. The effect can be a reminder of being present, of asking oneself "What exactly am I doing right now?" or "What exactly is going on around me right now?" One may therefore catch oneself doing things that make little sense, or suddenly become aware of something significant which has somehow eluded one's notice before. In this way the added layer of understanding/expectation/consciousness is not supposed to be defined by the preceding layer(s), but is to keep existence in a state of suspension and uncertainty.

For Marcus Aurelius, one of the most important Stoic philosophers, the overlaying of different consciousnesses could help one to see things. The reflections that the emperor Marcus Aurelius wrote in Greek in the second century A.D. show various approaches in attending an exact perception of things. Among them is a passage related to the robe of purple:

> Surely it is an excellent plan, when you are seated before delicacies and choice foods, to impress upon your imagination that this is the dead body of a fish, that the dead body of a bird or a pig; and again, that the Falernian wine is grape juice and that robe of purple a lamb's fleece dipped in a shell-fish's blood; and in matters of sex intercourse, that it is attrition of an entrail and a convulsive expulsion of mere mucus. Surely these are excellent imaginations, going to the heart of actual facts and penetrating them so as to see what kind of things they really are. You should adopt this practice all through your life, and where things make an impression which is very plausible, uncover their nakedness, see into their cheapness, strip off the profession on which they vaunt themselves (*Meditations, 6.13*).

Establishing the causal aspects of the unique position represented by purple in this way demystifies its regal symbolism. This impassioned and detached gaze, in revealing things "as they really are", is also an estranged one. The estranged gaze dilutes the nobility of purple; likewise it can dilute the Confucian negative attitude toward purple. What Marcus Aurelius did was to exercise intellect and rationality as a way to stay detached and objective, so as to escape the constraints of conventional, inert thinking. This has also encouraged my employment of pixilation. With the live actor being manipulated frame by frame, the pixilated figure is in a state between an autonomous being and a passive puppet. Through the hybridised figure (and the scene of telepathic connection between the drawn and the cinematographic), the practice seeks to call into question the boundaries that differentiate and distinguish meanings such as truth and fiction, subject and object, as well as the original and the remake. As Trahair (1991: 205) puts it from a post-structuralist perspective: "At the very moment of its epistemological emergence, the original must always disappear; and with the disappearance of the original comes that of the remake". The status of the hybridised figure, as shown in the pixilated efforts in the practice of this project, is not a valorised one. Their presence invokes the double, a sort of spattered mess, and uncanniness. What they seek to present is the illusiveness of representation, just like what Chuang-tzu recognised in the interchangibility of reality, and what Marcus Aurelius intended to do in untying one's thinking from stasis and inanimate conventions.

Looking at the world from an estranged perspective can be achieved by mixing it with angles of otherness such as puppet, insect and foreigner. For an animator, the animated is otherness. The practice of this project integrates the consciousnesses of the animator and the animated through the operation of materiality. This kind of integration may be estranged for me and for what I see in mainstream cinema, yet it may not be so for experimental animation. For the world of experimental animation, one might even say it has become a kind of frequent expression since there are numerous experiments in integrating the consciousness of the animator and that of the animated (for example in *Animated Self-Portraits* by 27 animators, 1989). My contribution, I would hope, is that I make a point of drawing on the performance of the interface between live action and animation to create this assemblage of layered consciousnesses. Although the interweaving of the animator and the animated may have become a kind of trope, through exploring the interface and the effect of estrangement it brings about, this interweaving or integration can produce something different. Nevertheless it is all very much context dependent, just like the way that poetry using extremely difficult language may have become too familiar for some people. Jan Mukarovsky, the early Czech structuralist, points out that strangeness can become automatised within a particular cultural context (Burbank and Steiner 1977). The reality or artistic conventions that the filmmaker aims to defamiliarise evolve all the time; there can hardly be obvious rules for estrangement. Most independent filmmakers would like to produce something entirely new or different, but the effect of estrangement is always going to be a subjective response on the part of the viewer, i.e. it is difficult to be objectively assessed. Therefore in the following section I consider this approach from the message it delivers, asking the question "how does it matter" rather than "how strange is it".

2.3 Derealising Hyperrealism

In this section I explain the messages I wish to deliver when exploring the effect of estrangement. Derealisation is a term often used to describe the dissociative symptom related to psychiatric and neurological disorders, in which one perceives or experiences an alteration of the external world that induces feelings of unreality and derealises the outside world. In the field of literary criticism and philosophy Jean-Paul Sartre refers to derealisation as an effect resulting from the desire to escape from reality, and the use of the imagination (Sartre 2004: [1978]). Fredric Jameson mentions it when illustrating the side effect of hyperreality (1991: 19). In this project I use this term to indicate an estrangement that is more concerned with the message, i.e. the meaning, than the aesthetic effect.

The technique of pixilation, or the integration of live actor and stop-frame photography, is central to my exploration of estrangement. In this project there are four kinds of such integration. The first appears in *Nothing to Do with Weather* (fig. 2-3), where the live actor repeats the process of moving a little bit, pausing and taking a photo to present *ordinary* actions. The second is a typical example of pixilation, where the live actor makes absurd poses and is photographed. As seen in the end scenes of *Animating Animator the Animated* (fig. 2-4), the resulting photo sequences present movement that is impossible in ordinary life. In *Animating Animator the Animated* and *Flying Tunes* there are two attempts to integrate pixilation and cartoon's hyperrealism. The two integrations are an attempt to estrange, derealise cartoon's hyperrealism. As an important part of this project, these two kinds of integration are discussed in detail in Chapter 4.

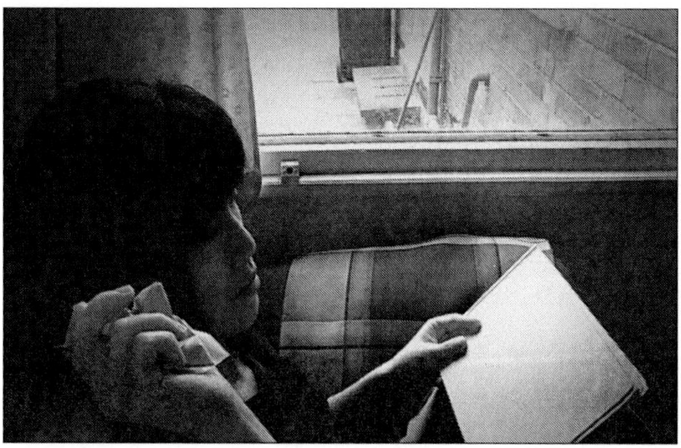

Fig. 2-3: Stop-frame photography in Nothing to Do with Weather.

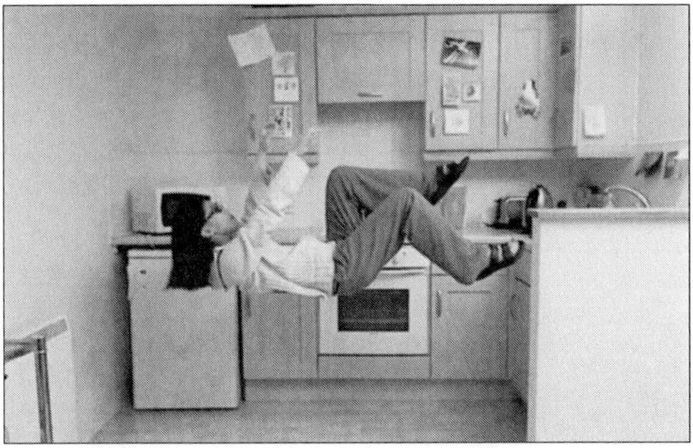

Fig. 2-4: Pixilation in the end scenes of Animating Animator the Animated.

In exploiting the effect of estrangement, this project explores a simple metaphor: all the animators in the world are puppets of Hollywood mainstream cinema. This section proceeds from the discussion of the origin of cartoon's hyperrealism and its influence on hybrid film. The development of cartoon's hyperrealism is connected to the industrialisation of animated films and also to the dominance of the Hollywood cartoon film in the non-Western world. In accounts of hyperrealism, there is scarcely a mention of the Far East. However, as a Far-eastern Asian, my practice inevitably reflects my cultural identity. Divorcing my thinking from a Far-Eastern standpoint seems unlikely. The practice of this project is to some extent to offer a visual account of the condition of a Far-Eastern animator. My account of cartoon's hyperrealism in this section will therefore include a description of the situation in the Far East, an aspect that is estranged in the dominant narrative of cartoon's hyperrealism. And in my practice, since the perfection of cartoon's hyperrealism is responsible for the seemingly unshakable leading-position of Hollywood animated films, cartoon's hyperrealism becomes something this project wishes to derealise.

Cartoon's Hyperrealism

Both Eco and Baudrillard have taken the Disneyland theme park as an exemplar of hyperreality. Actually, when put in the context of animation, the term "hyperrealism" has a very different meaning, which often used to describe the "realistic" cartoon style developed by Disney animators. As Lister *et al.* (2008: 138) point out, "[i]t is used to identify a distinct and dominant aesthetic in popular animation, developed by the Disney

Company in their animated feature films, beginning with *Snow White and the Seven Dwarfs* in 1937." Cartoon's hyperrealist approach in a sense is based on live-action convention for it presents its characters and environments as broadly conforming to the physics of the real world. This set of principles is most fully realised through hand-drawn animation, but they also have been widely used by non-drawn animation to achieve the "cartooniness" of hand-drawn animation. Today, most people's idea of cartoon animation relates to works that are in line with hyperrealism. Yet this was not the case in the early days. Think of the works made by Emile Cohl, the Fleischer brothers, or the first cartoon star Felix the Cat, we would find very different aesthetics where unconstrained movement, metamorphosis and anarchic dynamics characterised and vitalised those early cartoon. As for the development of the hyperrealist approach, it is generally considered to begin with Walt Disney's attempt to produce his first cartoon feature film *Snow White and the Seven Dwarfs*. To keep the audience absorbed and interested in "drawings" for over an hour, the Disney Company gave up the "plasmaticness" quality praised by Eisenstein (1987: 21) in their early works, and introduced the codes and ideologies of live-action cinema into this originally quite avant-garde inclined form. As a creative imitation of the real world, cartoon's hyperrealism has a lot to do with principles of movement, yet it is also about fantastic subject matter, such as talking animals, fairy tales and monsters (Lister *et al.* 2008: 138), and a clear, positive and logical storyline. It is powerful in creating a convincing fantastic world. Under this set of principles, even the Fleischer brothers' rotoscoping, a technique characterised by its ability to produce effects that intrigued the audience, was tamed and turned into something that fit perfectly into the fantasy, fairy-tale world. In *Snow White and the Seven Dwarfs*, the milestone of cartoon's hyperrealism, rotoscoping was employed for the heroine herself: the actress was filmed and then the individual frames were used to trace over. Full rotoscoping would surely be a problem in terms of Disney-esque hyperrealism. Disney's leading animators Frank Thomas and Ollie Johnston (1981: 323) recall their experience that "…whenever we stayed too close to the Photostats [produced by rotoscope], or directly copied even a tiny piece of human action, the result looked very strange. The moves appeared real enough, but the figure lost the illusion of life". Disney animators had to re-interpret the live performances and redrew the photographs in "animatable shapes" to "idealise the real" to get "the illusion of life". As a result, the fusion of captured performance and animator's interpretation was smooth and sophisticated, like a flawlessly glossy apple. Unlike the Koko the Clown films, where surreal results were produced due to discord between live action and drawn form, the *Snow White* film reproduced a prominently elegant fantasy through a highly harmonised style.

The principle of hyperrealism guided Disney's approach to integrating live action and animation. With hyperrealism, the task of hybrid films is not just to build a sweeter, funnier fantastic world that is parallel to ours. It is more about the bridge between these two, making the audience believe that the fantastic world is really accessible. In fact, Disney did not show much ambition for hybrid films in the early years. After the success of his 1920s "Alice series", a series of hybrid shorts combining a live-action girl and cartoon background, he made no other significant works in this way for a long time. A hybrid approach became attractive to Disney again because of World War II, since "budgets had become tighter, many skilled animators had been lost to the war effort, and the studio had committed much of its remaining resources to producing training and informational films for the government" (Telotte 2010: 143). By incorporating live-action elements, animators could draw fewer images, thus reducing cost or production time. These hybrid efforts, including films like *The Three Caballeros* (1945), *Song of the South* (1946), and *Fun and Fancy Free* (1947), were called "package pictures" for none of them maintained a single narrative, but instead they combined a variety of pieces into one feature-length film. As pursued by Disney, these films, although composed of fragments and heterogeneous materials, endeavoured to blur the boundaries. To achieve an integral visual design scheme, as Thomas and Johnston (1981: 524-25) explain, "The real parts were theatrical sets and had been designed with flat surfaces and simple shapes so they would match the drawings that had to be part of the whole composition". Their techniques were sophisticated enough that the viewer can hardly tell where is the border between live-action and animated part. As the visual borders get dissolved, the real and the fantastic world also seem to fuse up. Telotte (2010: 152) argues that the world shown in these films is not simply our own "laughing place"; it is the space of imagination, a more promising world that invites us to challenge the topography of the real world – "a world of fences, economic barriers, racial prejudice, and cultural boundaries". This kind of endeavour was continued in Disney's hybrid works in the later years, including *Mary Poppins* (1964), the most Oscar-nominated Disney film in history, and *Enchanted* (2007), a more recent hybrid effort that was successful in terms of both critical reception and box office receipts. For Telotte (2010: 176), the aim of the highly harmonised, idealised world is to invite audiences to step from the imperfect real world into a wonderful animated one, and then bring its blessings back to the real world. In my view, the effect may actually be the opposite for some. It is just as likely to emphasise a growing sense of distance between the central and the marginal, as well as an increasing alienation between animation artists and their works.

Cartoon's Live Action Dream?

Cartoon's hyperrealism is arguably the product of a compromise of animation with live action – animation's dream of achieving the status of live action, partly through becoming visually similar to it. In the early stages of cartoon's realist approaches, the observation of the real world was very much valued in Disney's studio. The animators had to undertake programmes of training in the skills and techniques of fine art for greater notions of realism (Telotte 2010: 12). While believing that they maintain a hyperrealism that is "neither a completely accurate version of the real world nor a radical vindication of the animated form" (Wells 1998: 25), the verisimilitude they pursued in the films is an imitation of the real. This kind of approach was actually animation's attempt, after being marginalised for decades in the early twentieth century, to legitimise itself in terms of Hollywood mainstream cinema. Friz Freleng's *You Ought to Be in Pictures* (1940) is a classic example reflecting the status of animation versus live action at that period. In this hybrid film, the action takes place against a "real" background, i.e. the real office of the producer Leon Schlesinger, the real lot of the Warner Bros. Studio, and the actual Los Angles traffic, with all the characters real people except Porky Pig and Daffy Duck. It is lunch-time, and the animators have all left the studio. Daffy, framed in a picture hanging on the wall, starts to speak. He persuades Porky who is resting in an animation paper on a drawing desk to resign from the cartoon studios to pursue a career in feature films, "as Bette Davis' leading man, at three grand a week". Porky is lured and goes to Leon Schlesinger asking to have his contract torn up. He then starts trying to get into the studio to play a live action role. To get access to live action is not an easy thing, not even disguised as Oliver Hardy. In the end, the discouraged Porky goes back to see if Schlesinger will take him back, and finds that Daffy is trying to convince Schlesinger that he should take over Porky's roles. Nonetheless, Schlesinger has been waiting for Porky's return. Porky finally can go back into the animation paper that he was in, happily and contentedly.

With a photographed cut-out of a real hand that is being animated along with a depiction of the cartoon character Porky that introduces him as a drawing on the animator's drawing board, it could be inferred that both the drawn and the live are at a level similarly constructed. This metaphor is further enhanced in the following scenes: the cartooning of the live-action animators when they leave the studio in a flock; the juxtaposition of portraits of both drawn and real figures in Schlesinger's office; the caricaturing of the studio guard, who is given an exaggerated voice by the cartoon voice artist Mel Blanc; and the production of highly artificial world of a Busby Berkeley-style musical which Porky watches in the studio. The fact that even the cartoon character wants to change his career pathway to live-action feature suggests the pre-eminence of live-action cinema over cartoon animation. The creation of feature-length cartoons was supposed to be an antidote to animation's marginalised position. However its pursuit of higher status in mainstream cinema seemed to involve sacrifice. *Snow White and the Seven Dwarfs* "caused Disney to massify production, occasioning the move to a 24-hour factory of distraction production" (Leslie 2004: 135), and turned animation production into an extreme division of labour. Following Disney, many companies divided the labour of animation and standardised the output. The industrialised animation is not the world of Gertie, Felix or Koko where the artifice of screen and the reality are used to be provoked or played with. There were few possibilities for spontaneous invention and the individualistic nature of animation was conceded to collective production.

Cartoon's Hyperrealism and Asian Cartoon Industry

Nevertheless, the success of *Snow White and the Seven Dwarfs* reinforced Disney's leading position in Hollywood as well as the whole world. The year *Snow White* released was 1936. In Asia the greatest military conflict between China and Japan started in 1937. In the ensuing decade China was engaged in a devastating war with Japan, and much of the country was under Japanese control until the end of World War II, and the film industry suffered a radical decline. The Wan brothers who had already long been established as pioneering animators in China saw Disney's *Snow White* in Shanghai and were determined to produce something of a similarly high standard. The result was China's first feature-length animated film *Princess Iron Fan* (1941), which was also the first traditionally-animated feature in Asia. These two "princess" films were both adapted from well-known stories. While *Snow White and the Seven Dwarfs* was based on the famous European fairy tale collected and retold by Brothers Grimm,*Princess Iron Fan* was a character from *Journey to the West*, a classic sixteenth-century Chinese novel that has inspired numerous adaptations in traditional opera and story-telling activity. The novel recounts the legendary pilgrimage to India of the Buddhist monk Xuanzang and his three protectors – Sun Wukong the Monkey King, Zhu Bajie the Pig and human monk ShaWujing. In this particular section of the story, the pilgrims find their passage blocked by a flame-engulfed mountain ruled over by a fiery demon. The flames can only be dampened by a mythical fan in the possession of a princess, but her son happens to have been killed by Monkey King in a previous incident, and she is in no mood to lend the pilgrims her legendary fan. Unlike the Western fairy-tale tradition, a "princess" character is quite rare in Chinese folklore, and Princess Iron Fan might be the only one that most people think of. Choosing this particular piece of story seems to be in response to Snow White the princess. Influenced by *Snow White and the Seven Dwarfs*, *Princess Iron Fan* became a curious - if not strange - mix of Western style of caricature and traditional Chinese visual expression. For example, Hollywood cartoon's surreal approaches such as metamorphosis and flexible bodies are mixed with the traditional acting style of Beijing Opera; Monkey King is a combination of Beijing Opera facial makeup and the "rubber-hose" limbs common in early Hollywood cartoons. Some of the character design is based on that of Chinese shadow puppet plays, while some others resemble real people or Hollywood cartoon stars. The character Pretty Face Fox, who is supposed to be the prettiest woman in the film, looks completely different to all the other female characters including Princess Iron Fan. With the peak on the forehead, shiny eyelids, long eyelashes, and a baby face, Pretty Face Fox is very reminiscent of Betty Boop (fig. 2-5). The sound track is also a strange hybrid. Buddhist music is interestingly put side by side with sound effects common in Hollywood cartoons, yet the clumsy application of sound effects is a bit confusing, e.g. the sound effect for Monkey King flying into the skyis a sound recognisable from Hollywood cartoons that indicates the action of falling. It is therefore sometimes perplexing for a viewer who is familiar with Hollywood cartoons to understand what is really going on due to the conflict between sound effects and actions.

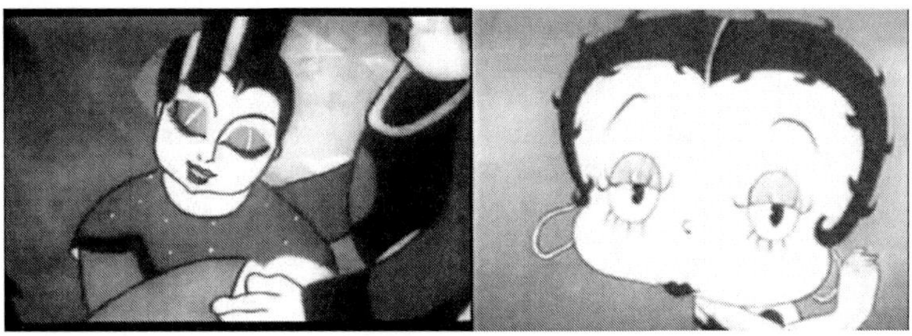

Fig. 2-5: Pretty Face Fox (left) and Betty Boop (right)

Apart from the misleading sound effects, in my view the scenes depicting Monkey King's first attempt to pass through the flaming mountain is the most creative and inventive part. However the film is crude in many places. The movements represented by the frame-by-frame drawings are awkwardly unstable. Rotoscoping was used extensively, probably due to the low budget, yet the juxtaposition of caricaturised performance and the unrefined rotoscoping figures makes it an even clumsier work.

Snow White and the Seven Dwarfs not only demonstrated Disney's cutting-edge technological achievements, but also proved cartoon's ability to build a convincing world that is as powerful as a live-action film in terms of creating emotional involvement on the part of the audience. In contrast, *Princess Iron Fan* consistently disrupted the persuasiveness of the screened world by putting together a bundle of inconsistent visual qualities. It unfortunately looks more like a lumpish imitation of the Hollywood counterparts than an aesthetic challenge to them.

Despite all this, *Princess Iron Fan* was a box office success in Shanghai. The incorporation of folk-art-style character design and Chinese landscape painting in the background earned it a lot of praise. Obviously the achievement of these two films should be considered with regard to their respective contexts – i.e. industrial, political, technological and cultural. While the quality of *Princess Iron Fan* could not measure up to its Hollywood counterparts, its accomplishment should not be downplayed, especially in the view of the circumstances under which this film was made. Its influences were also far-reaching. The film's export to Japan in 1942 was the start of the revolution of Japanese animation: first, it led to the government commissioning the country's first animated feature, the propaganda film *Momotaro's Divine Sea Warrior* (1945). Second and most importantly, it encouraged fourteen-years-old Osamu Tezuka – the godfather of manga and creator of Astro Boy and Kimba the White Lion – to pick up his pen and drew his first hit comics (Tezuka 1989).

While the history of Japanese animation began at the start of the 20th century, the characteristic anime style developed in the 1960s with the work of Osamu Tezuka. To meet the realities of low budgets, tight schedules and inexperienced animation-staff, Tezuka adapted and simplified many Disney animation techniques to reduce costs and to limit the number of frames in production. Instead of striving for sophisticated full animation, he put more effort into telling an intense and appealing story. He intended this simplification as a temporary measure, but found it to be so successful that he continued with the process. He established many of the features of today's Japanese anime. As Tezuka had been a great fan of Disney animation from a very young age, he was greatly influenced both by Betty Boop and many of Disney's films – especially *Bambi*, which he reported he had seen no less than a hundred times (Lent 2000). It was surely Hollywood cartoons that played a pivotal role in the formative years of his concept of animation, but it was *Princess Iron Fan* that encouraged him to pursue something different from Disney. He states in an interview: "This film [Princess Iron Fan] is brilliant. Watching it is like meeting the next-door neighbour who makes you feel close and familiar" (video clip exhibited in the Tezuka Osamu Memorial Museum). It was perhaps a cultural affinity he felt with the film. While on a visit to China in 1959,

Tezuka met Wan Laiming and expressed his appreciation. During their meeting they collaborated to draw a picture of Astro Boy and Monkey King together. The series of "Astro Boy' subsequently became the most influential anime in China.

The interplay between foreign and indigenous animation is evident across East Asia and has affected many of its premier animators. Aside from the Wan brothers and Tezuka, other pioneering animators who have talked about being enamoured with Hollywood cartoons include James Wang of Taiwan with *Bambi*, Payut Ngaokrachang of Thailand with *Snow White* and other works featuring Felix the Cat, and A Da of China with *Snow White* (Lent 2000). These Asian pioneers: Ngaokrachang of Thailand, Tezuka of Japan, and Shin Dong Hun of Korea, all proudly accepted the title given to them by journalists and cartoon fans as "The Disney" of their respective countries. Wang's Wang Film Productions Co., the biggest animation studio in Taiwan, has also enjoyed being named as "Asia's Disney" (Chang 1998).

Animated Filmmaking as a Hyperrealistic Dream in Asia

Apart from being inspired by, and aspiring to, the achievements of Hollywood cartoons, Asia's animation production has long attracted foreign interests due to its stable and inexpensive labour supplies. Since the 1960s, Hollywood studios have established and maintained production facilities, first in Japan, then in South Korea and Taiwan, and now also in the Philippines, Malaysia, Singapore, Vietnam, Thailand, India, Indonesia and China. The financial concerns of the industry made it practical for Asia to feed the cartoon world, to the extent that today, about 90% of all "American" television animation is physically produced in Asia (Pesimo 2007: 124), i.e. much of the labour is outsourced. Asian animation companies bid enthusiastically for this global business pie, believing that it provides employment and skills for young people, brings in foreign capital, and facilitates the creation of domestic animation. Offshore animation does lead to the creation and nurturing of local industry, yet it does not seem to offer much help to the growth of domestic animation in these countries. Foreign-based studios are not interested in developing animation that meets local needs or interests. As for outsourced service providers, they foster manpower in drawing, painting, inking and so forth. However, the most crucial part – the development of script, model sheets, storyboard, and the final editing – is normally carried out in Hollywood studios and has nothing to do with them. Without sufficient knowledge and experience, their attempts to produce an animated feature independently often meet with failure. Even if they have succeeded in producing a few, the films are often disdained as low-quality by its domestic audience who have grown up watching Hollywood cartoons. This is exactly the current situation in Taiwan.

From the mid-1980s, Taiwan's animation industry has relied heavily on providing outsourced service for Hollywood cartoons. At Wang Film productions Co., annual production reached nearly 200 cartoons a year (Tsai 2006: 13). Although the industry grew rapidly over this period, with a great amount of Hollywood and Japanese cartoons made in Taiwan, the films they made for foreign bosses were quickly sold back to Taiwan and resulted in the flooding of the domestic market. In the end no home-made cartoon appeared on TV channels at all. Despite decades of hard work and several ambitious attempts, Taiwan's animation studios have not yet figured out how to create an animated feature that is able to compete in both the domestic and global markets. Unable to make money on home production, outsourced service is still the most reliable source of profit. Under such circumstances, animators are pretty much like factory workers. The main difference is that one needs to be very skilful to be qualified for an animation factory. Surveys by Taiwan's Council of Labor Affairs (2012) have shown that animators in Taiwan start on very poor salaries, which are less than restaurant employee wages. Even when they have worked for several years and become experienced animators, the average salary is still much lower than the average national income in Taiwan. Low wages are not uncommon for animators in East Asia. In Japan the situation is even worse. Anime animators are noted for their long-hours and low-pay conditions. Animation jobs require quite high-level skills. To get an animation job, one has to study animation for several years in school, and work hard to become skilled enough to have the chance to be employed. However, an anime animator often earns less than he/she would doing a part-time job in a convenience store. As a result, animators in Japan often live in such poverty that nearly forty percent of them are not able to afford basic healthcare coverage, according to a survey based on at least 700 anime producers and directors (Kelts 2009).

Even with such poor working conditions, animation still attracted an unprecedentedly large number of young people. When I was a graduate student in Taiwan, I worked in a private animation training school as a teaching assistant. There I noticed a particular phenomenon; people who signed up for the private animation courses came from all walks of life. Most of them had never taken any courses related to art or design when they were in university. Allured by the Hollywood digital films they saw in the cinema, they quit their original jobs and took those expensive continuation courses, hoping to be engaged in a creative career like animation. But none of them realised that animation jobs in Taiwan are not so creative. In the end, most of the students disappointedly went back to their original jobs. The days of pursuing animation career were like having a dream, a dream that is supported by the perfect illusion created by Hollywood mainstream animations. Cartoon's hyperrealism has played a crucial part in facilitating this dream world. Yet, as illustrated earlier, it is itself a product of dreaming of achieving live action's status, an illusion created by cartoon's otherness. In the end, could it be that everyone is living in dreams that may be too real to be dreams any more?

Evolving from activities such as optical toys and vaudeville lightning sketches, the art of the moving image in the West can be considered to have developed in a gradual and consistent history. In East Asia, having no such similar illusionist tradition in the past, the art of the moving image was a concept without roots, a practice without a philosophy. From the story of the birth of China's first feature animation, it seems reasonable to say that the pursuit of animated film in China was destined to be a struggle between imitation and reaction. Western, and specifically Hollywood, cultural dominance in the area of cinema forms a crucial framework for the understanding of film production in East Asia. As film critics Roy Armes (1987: 35) points out,

> Whatever cinema may have become with the passing of time, its emergence cannot be ascribed solely to artistic aspiration or disinterested scientific endeavour. Unlike the later systems of radio and television broadcasting, the cinema has not been a tool or direct expression of the state: as a "free enterprise" system, its inception and development are closely tied to the profit motive as it is expressed in and through Western capitalism.

The consequence of the local audience's taste being shaped by foreign films should not be neglected. In Taiwan and China, the attempt to make an animated feature with a Chinese identity usually results in a hybrid product – part-indigenous, part-Westernised – that does not correspond to local audience's tastes. In Andy Huang's hybrid work *Doll Face* (2005), the machine struggles to construct its own identity by mimicking images presented on a television screen. The unattainable goals eventually lead to the machine's self-deconstruction. The plot seems pertinent to East Asia's pursuit to live up to the western standard for a perfect animation. Even so, any pursuit in real life is really a much more complex and opaque process.

Because of the fear of Chinese communism, Marxism was banned in Taiwan for most of the twentieth century. Its fundamental texts remained notorious for a long time after the ban was lifted in the end of last century. In the *Economic and Philosophical Manuscripts* of 1844 Karl Marx discusses the problem of alienation that workers will suffer in industrial production under capitalist conditions. The four types of alienation identified by him all seem to be relevant to the conditions of animators in industrialised era – first, alienation of the worker from the work he produces or the product of his labour; second, alienation of the worker from working or the act of producing itself; third, alienation of the worker from himself as a producer; and last, alienation of the worker from other workers or producers. When I read this, just after having come to Europe, I was astonished by Marx's description of the types of alienation: it has so many parallels to the condition of Taiwan's animators today. The tension between what is avoided and what is happening is intriguing. Now I am here, trying to understand, interpret and practice the idea of moving image using concepts from Western thinkers like Freud, Shklovsky and even Aurelius the Roman emperor. When I am thinking about derealising the screened world, the dream world provided by Western visual technology, I am relying heavily on Western paradigms. However, am I really talking about Freud, Shklovsky and Aurelius, or am I just borrowing their words to voice something they did not mean? In the beginning of this section I mentioned the metaphor about all the animators in the world being the puppets of Hollywood mainstream cinema. It sounds quite straightforward on the surface. Yet is a puppeteer really that far from a puppet, or is a puppet also a puppeteer in some way? Isn't Asia's endeavour to Westernise Asian concepts also an endeavour to Asianise Western concepts? So this is what has been implied in the practice of this study – a description of liminal experiences – through the operation of materiality, and the manoeuvre of estrangement.

CHAPTER THREE

ESTRANGED SUBJECTIVITY

All approaches stressed in this research such as defamiliarisation, estrangement and derealisation as discussed in the previous chapter are related to the sense of existence of the on-screen characters, which can be used by filmmakers to express issues regarding subjectivity, selfhood and identity in the real world. Subjectivity is one of the core themes in the practice of this research. This is evidenced in three respects. Firstly, the three films all concern relations between the creator and the creation, manipulating and being controlled, and the relations between individuals and external forces such as fate or society. Secondly, the fact that I have inserted/presented myself (the author/actor) in two of the films raises the issue of self-representation, the identity of the animator, and the representation of filmmaking practice. Here self-figuration in the practice can be the demonstration of the animator's awareness of his/her creative self and cultural background. Finally, all three films give weight to the design and performance of hybridised characters, which have been explored in terms of their capacity to interrogate the construction of subjectivity. This chapter proposes that subjectivity is an effective trope for investigating the formal manipulation of the integration between live action and animation. In my practice both the creator and the created have unstable and interchangeable subjectivities. This understanding of subjectivity has been greatly influenced by the experience of studying and living abroad, i.e. it draws attention to the cultural differences and their impact on the subject's identity and experience of the world; therefore in this chapter I will start the discussion by outlining these experiences under the heading "Studying abroad and personal subjectivity". The performance of subjectivity in my practice will then be investigated via three topics: (1) the contest between autonomy and subjection in hybrid work, (2) representation of filmmaking practice, and (3) hybridised character and estranged subjectivity.

In the previous chapter, the "distinction" between the subject and object was questioned. As subjectivity is explored in some depth in my practice, this chapter continues the discussion of self-other demarcation and individual identity, from the suspension of self-other opposition to their co-existence in a single entity. The hybridised characters are used to embody this co-existence, so as to achieve an estranged subjectivity.

3.1 Studying Abroad and Personal Subjectivity

> "Experience is a hard teacher because she gives the test first, the lesson afterwards."
> —Vernon Law (Nathan 2000)

Before I came to the UK, subjective consciousness was not a significant concern in my work. However, living abroad is often an experience that can heighten one's subjective consciousness. Studying and living in the UK has greatly raised my awareness of existential questions – and also caused me to question my cultural identity. It directly influenced my practice and research interest, and therefore I shall devote some space to describing the impact of living abroad on my idea of subjectivity.

I come from a society that is quite homogenous compared to the UK which is much more multi-cultural in its population. So I was shocked to find how often I was attacked on the street, physically and verbally. It made me feel an unwelcome foreigner. Yet the most disturbing experience, other than this kind of harassment, is the kind that negates my identity – as a Taiwanese.

This is demonstrated by one example that occurred during the writing up of this thesis, when the London Olympics were in full flow. The flags of 206 nations were exhibited in Piccadilly Circus. As a participant, it would seem perfectly normal that Taiwan's flag was included. Yet the appearance of Taiwan's red, blue and white emblem attracted Taiwanese tourists and students to take photographs of it, and even made media headlines in Taiwan. Three days later, Taiwan's flag was removed from this public display at the suggestion of The Foreign Office because of its concern about upsetting China.

To most Westerners, Taiwan is indistinguishable from (mainland) China, hence the detailed background given here. Few Westerners know the tortured history of Taiwan's relations with mainland China. My home nation is the Republic of China, or RoC. But the name Taiwan or RoC is not allowed to appear in most international environments. Due to China's intervention, the island state of 23 million people is obliged to participate in international events under a made-up name, with a similarly artificial flag and anthem. Moreover, not every made-up name is allowed. To satisfy China, it has to be a name that sounds ambiguous enough to be more like a province than a country, a name like "Chinese Taipei".

Beijing views Taiwan as an upstart renegade province to be reintegrated, by force if necessary. The dispute between Taiwan and Beijing is actually a fight between two different systems of government.[3] Beijing believes in a one-party dictatorship, while Taiwan became a democracy decades ago. Although RoC was one of the founding members of the United Nations, when the PRC became powerful enough, the UN quickly switched its recognition to PRC and expelled the RoC. Now the island country is politically isolated.[4] Any country or international organisation that recognises Taiwan as an independent country will be punished by China. Who wants to be an opponent of China now?[5]

China's constant and brutal suppression of the democratic movement figures, religious activists and Tibet's endeavour for freedom repeatedly reminds the Taiwanese that their welfare is highly vulnerable. Although this is the reality that I have always known, nothing upset me more than my first encounter with people from mainland China in the UK.[6] For them it was their first encounter with a Taiwanese too, as communications between Taiwan and China were still fairly limited before I came to the UK. We treated each other politely, and although we did not socialise

---

[3]RoC was the name given to mainland China in 1911 by the Nationalists, to mark their overthrowing of the last feudal dynasty, the Qing, and ending imperialism in China. After World War II, when the Nationalists had just finished an exhausting seven-year battle with Japan, Chinese Communists took advantage, defeated the nationalistic army and took control of mainland China. While the Communists declared the People's Republic of China (PRC) as the successor state to RoC, the Nationalists managed to keep Taiwan and used the name of the RoC, in the belief that they would soon return to power on the mainland, and were perpetuating the 'true' name of China. From then on Taiwan seemed to be destined for a bitter existence.

[4] Taiwan does not even have the status of "observer" in the UN and is only recognised as a nation by about two dozen nations such as Palau, Kiribati and Swaziland. Everyone else, even its close ally America, must officially pretend otherwise.

[5] The already very limited international recognition of Taiwan still irritates China. To further isolate Taiwan, for example, in 2002 it promised to pay the island nation of Nauru more than 130 million dollars to change their diplomatic affairs from Taipei to Peking; and Nauru only has a population of fewer than 10,000 people. Taiwan can hardly cope with this process. It can only work hard to maintain a strong economic position in the region and thus continue to have relationships with other countries, even if only unofficially. But that takes a lot of energy and is a lonely, if not futile, task.

[6] We call mainland Chinese "China people" (中國人) rather than "Chinese people" (華人) because in Mandarin the words for these two terms are different. The former indicates the nationality while the latter can be used for people from Singapore, Malaysia and any other country, as long as your ancient ancestor is from China.

much, we got together for a meal at Chinese New Year. In no time the conversation grew intense, and turned to Taiwan's national identity. I complained about China's rockets and threats.[7] One girl responded "If you refuse to admit your nationality is China, that Taiwan is part of China, you deserve to die." Even for these elite students who had never been tortured by poverty and had the chance to see the world, they hold a blind and profound faith in the authoritarian government which they believe will lead them to a powerful, great, united China. To realise this large and unified Chinese power, they believe that issues of human life, morality or justice are of no significance. They seemed to believe whole-heartedly in the fake history learned in their formal education, about the greatness of Chinese communism.

This conversation was upsetting and confusing. I began to wonder if my thoughts about democracy and human rights were actually a result of being brainwashed by Taiwan's government or America (which China people used to blame). I felt that there is no ultimate truth and no basic common values. The most powerful subject decides everything. A horse can be called a stag if you are someone powerful enough.[8]

Even worse, I began to wonder whether a belief in autocracy actually lay in my cultural genes. Their belief in a great China, instead of being a result of Communist dictatorship, might perhaps derive from their longing for someone powerful to follow. The paternal nature and Confucianism in Chinese culture seem perfect for Communist dictatorship. This made me suspect an inherent weakness in the Chinese culture I grew up in, and that the lack of reflective thinking may be rooted in anyone raised within Chinese conventions. For the first time I felt so bad about the Chinese blood in my veins. Since the blood was already in my body, it meant I could not avoid hating, and feeling alienated from, myself.

Thinking about this, I found my experience to be a sort of a microcosm of the condition of Taiwan. During my years of studying abroad, public sentiment in Taiwan changed. As China's power increased, the Chinese aspects glorified by Chinese Communists become problematic, even distasteful, for many Taiwaneses. Taiwan grew to loathe its own cultural identity, and became eager to erase its bonds with Chinese culture. Before

---

7 Around 1500 Chinese rockets are pointed at Taiwan (BBC news, 2009; *Chinatimes*, 2012), and the number is still growing despite Taiwan's current leading party showing great compliance to China. Taiwan is an independent nation, but the name "Republic of China" gives China all the chances to take advantage – to claim that Taiwan is part of China. However if a Taiwanese politician even proposes to hold a referendum on simply removing "China" from the name "Republic of China", mainland China declares it will retaliate, as it considers Taiwan to belong to "the People's Republic of China".

8 "Calling a stag a horse" is a proverb that derives from an ancient Chinese Story.

I left, the creative company where I worked was proud of its excellence at applying and transforming Chinese visual elements into fashionable creative productions. This excellence had now become politically inappropriate. Taiwan was experiencing an obvious and difficult change of self-identity. This is quite painful for a country that used to feel proud of its Chinese cultural roots and sees itself as a better China.

Not having suffered from the brutal Culture Revolution, Taiwan was the only community in the world that had carefully preserved the Chinese heritage, integrating and respecting Chinese culture in its formal education, and retaining traditional Chinese characters in its writing. In just a few short years, Chinese elements became disdained by many Taiwan people and politically unacceptable. The change was so rapid and profound that the Taiwanese were uprooted in terms of both identity and mentality. This reality revealed how problematic and precarious subjectivity could be. Precarious subjectivity makes you anxious. Yet being a Taiwanese implies that there is no other choice than staying in a state of suspension. Sometimes a Taiwanese has to short-circuit him or herself and simply live with a weakened sense of identity.

Mental resilience is arguably the most critical trait for the weak to survive. It is vital not to avoid discomfort but to learn to live with it. It is probably an instinctive need for people to avoid things that are out of hand. When living in my homeland, my instinct was to avoid the anxieties of life. For example, I changed my subject of study when it was "no longer ideal"; changed career path when it was "not cool enough"; and so forth. Surrounded by family and abundant social resources, it was so easy to avoid facing moments of stress. Choosing not to plunge into the river of anxiety, I did not get the chance to experience underwater, thus no chance to see the scenery on the other side. Living alone in the UK, what I used to avoid has become unavoidable.

As Bayne (2008: 197) points out, the nature of higher education embraces aspects of uncertainty, strangeness, disquietude and troublesomeness. Being an overseas Ph.D. student can possibly enhance these aspects. A typical British Ph.D. student in the humanities spends most of the time on intensive work for her/his dissertation. The whole process is seemingly less structured compared with American and many East-Asian systems where you have less freedom but more guidance throughout the research process. For an overseas Ph.D. student this means you would possibly have more difficulty in facing cultural differences, understanding the different expectations in higher educational systems, and solving communication problems caused by either language barriers or cultural differences. Such a way of living is inevitably uncomfortable and anxiety-inducing. However, the uncertainty foregrounded in the life of a Ph.D. student may not be totally negative. As Royle (2003: 52) points out, "[i]ntellectual uncertainty is not necessarily or simply a negative experience, a dead-end sense of not knowing or of indeterminacy. It is just as well an experience of something open, generative, exhilarating (the trembling of what remains undecidable)". In effect, many scholars, such as Barnett (2005, 2007), Perkins (2006), and Meyer and Land (2005a, 2005b), refer to the necessity of intellectual uncertainty as the basis of a high quality university education. Barnett (2005: 36) suggests that "a pedagogical achievement of higher education is that – on the student's part – of coming to live purposefully with anxiety". The notion of "troublesome knowledge", as Perkins (2005: 37) describes, is characterised by "ritual knowledge, inert knowledge, conceptually difficult knowledge, foreign knowledge, and tacit knowledge". For Meyer and Land (2005a: 9), such troublesome knowledge may induce in students a sense of anxiety and disorientation, appearing "counter intuitive, alien…, or incoherent"; and yet it also suggests the perception of the student undergoes a "significant shift…[which] may lead to a transformation of personal identity, a reconstruction of subjectivity" (ibid.: 7).

No doubt the experience can differ tremendously among individual students. In my personal experience, to survive a demanding period of study and a lonely life, I have had to be willing to live with uncertainty and to accept a state of suspension. When depressed, which may often occur in the pursuit of doctoral study for foreign students with a completely different cultural background, it is vital to have a more accepting stance for negative feelings to exist, so that they do not become emotional traps and diminish my ability to endure and grow. In an environment where the unwanted is unavoidable and inescapable, genuine growth may develop.

Interestingly enough, now my favourite friends here are all from mainland China. These experiences constantly complicate my sense of subjectivity. Not surprisingly it became a theme in my practice. The exploration of the relationship between live action and animation turned into stories of subjectivities of the live-action and drawn figures. "Drawing hand" seemed to be a nice way to begin a story of struggling subjectivity. Two works in my practice, *Nothing to Do with Weather* and *Animating Animator the Animated,* started in this way (fig. 3-1, 3-2). The first began with a girl drawing a girl in a sketchbook, and the latter with an animator creating figures on a pad of paper. For the live-action girl in *Nothing to Do with Weather*, there are connections and interactions between her and the drawn girl. For the live-action animator in *Animating Animator the Animated*, being the creator of animated figure, she is influenced and even assimilated by her creation without direct interaction.

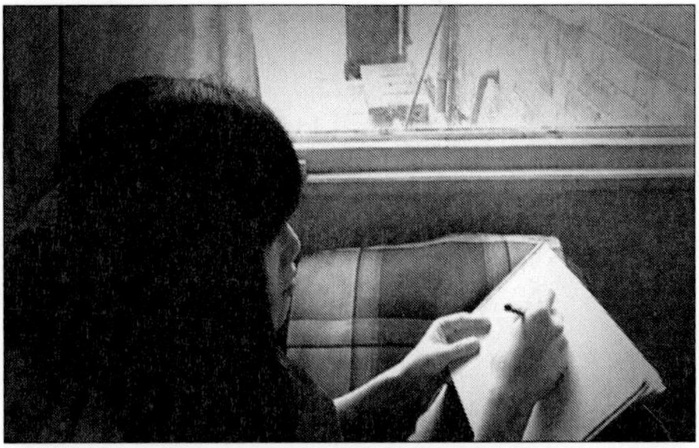

Fig. 3-1: "Drawing hand" in Nothing to Do with Weather

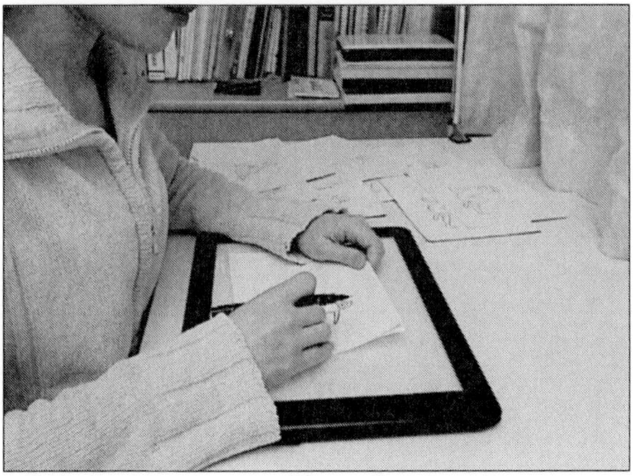

Fig. 3-2: "Drawing hand" in Animating Animator the Animated

Predictably, in my practice neither the creator (e.g. drawer, animator) or the created (e.g. the drawings, the animated) has a stable, self-sufficient subjectivity. Especially in *Animating Animator the Animated*, a work produced in the fifth year of my study, I wanted to make their subjectivities interchangeable and multi-layered as much as possible. Hybrid filmmaking seems to have great potential in exploring the theme of subjectivity. Examining historical works we can find that from the very beginning animated filmmakers extensively used hybrid works to explore their consciousness of creative subjectivity. While borrowing certain artistic devices from early animated films, my practice articulates the idea of a seemingly feeble and suppressed subjectivity. In my opinion, a diminished sense of ego actually can be – or even needs to be – the foundation for the cultivation of a resilient self and an appreciation of the connections between individuals. This diminished self is actually a result of the contests between autonomy and subjection within or between subjectivities. In the next section I will look at how historical hybrid films and my own practice present or reflect on these contests.

3.2 Subjectivity: Exhibition of the Context between Autonomy and Subjection

As discussed in Chapter 1, the concept of animation is strongly connected with the endowment of the quality of life. It can be argued that among all artistic forms, animation is most related to the idea of "life-giving". Crafton (1982: 6) asserts that animated cinema could not have existed before the cinema came into being around 1895, and that animation is a subspecies of film. Whether this latter claim is valid remains debatable, especially with the impact of digital tools. One thing that is certain is that the so-called *true* animation first appeared in the form of the hybrid of live action and animation with the "cooperation" of live action. The drawn sequences in J. Stuart Blackton's *Humorous Phases of Funny Faces* (1906) is often cited as the first example of true animated drawings (Beckerman 2003: 16), while the "first true animated cartoon" is generally understood to be *Fantasmagorie* made by French artist Emile Cohl in 1908 (Crafton 1982: 60). They both are manifestations of animation's specific association with life-giving. Both of the films begin with the artist's (photographic) hand at work. In general the live-action hands do two things: make or erase drawings, i.e. give or cancel life. The juxtaposition of live-action hands and moving drawings highlighted the difference between photographic images and drawings, and made it possible to understand animation as an aesthetic device.

Crafton (1982: 11) notes the concept of "self-figuration" as the tendency of filmmakers to interject themselves into their films in the early twentieth century. The presence of the animator invested early hybrid films with a quality of reflexiveness which speaks to the autonomy and subjection of the drawn figures, and presented a kind of "class struggle" between the animator and the animated. Through the intervention of the artist's hand, the knowing play with surface and depth, and the set-up of simulation and situation, early animators revealed the derivation of life on the screen. The intention to foreground the drawings, rather than the artist as an actor, has conferred on the animator an unusual role as the life giver, the magician who has the power to endow drawings with "the magic ability to move, spontaneously change their shape, or become "real" (three-dimensional)" (Crafton 1982: 50). An animator plays the role of the almighty hand, trifling with the creation under the pen. Meanwhile, these drawings are unwilling to be passive creatures only, they resist and oppose, striving to earn their own existence and independence. Most often these early hybrid films did not have linear or well-developed storylines. The relationship between the creator and the creation – the omnipotence of the animator's hand and the reaction of the drawn creation – was the main source of entertainment. The comment made by Gilbert Seldes in 1932 in the newspaper *The New Republic* makes it clear by describing the fascination of early animation as the fascination of magic, which states, "something in the form itself is a satisfaction to us. …In the early days we looked at a movie and marvelled that a picture could be set into motion. Now we do not think of the picture – only the actors. The animated cartoon shows us in movement something naturally inert, and it is essentially the satisfaction of magic that we get out of it" (cited in Crafton 1982: 12). Showing only hands, the animator was pictured as a powerful magician, and was implied to be the master of the universe created for the screen, claiming his animated figures' submission.

Today with digital technology it is too easy to create any kind of moving images. The audiences' mind-set toward moving images is different from that of the early twentieth century. The animated movement on the screen is no longer magical, but simply the product of skilled technicians and/or expensive software. However, as a critical element of the art of moving images, it is meaningful to renew the representation and the "magic" of movement, especially when naturalism and "audience involvement" (Johnston & Thomas, 1981) has become so dominant in mainstream cinema. There are at least two ways to draw the audiences' attention to the movement: one is to extremely exaggerate it; the other is to hybridise it so as to create formal interruption. I chose the latter since at the same time it demonstrates my attitude that there is no single core for subjectivity in the world. In *Nothing to Do with Weather* I tried two tentative methods for hybridised movement. The first is to represent the live-action girl's movement by still photographs. The second is to create the drawn girl's movement in the running scene with simple geometric shapes, using 3-D computer software, and then tracing it onto paper so that the drawn girl becomes a combination of drawings and three-dimensional animation. These experiments helped me to identify the estranging potential of hybridised movements to explore issues of autonomy and subjection.

The magic of movement is important for the genesis theme in early hybrid films. Apart from that, regarding the depictions of the relationship between animator and the animated in early hybrid films, there is another tendency worth noticing. In these films, although animators enjoy a privileged role as the creators of life, their personalities were not particularly explored, i.e. they had little other role than that of the master-creator. Drawings created by them are the real centre of the limelight, playing out dramas of self-struggle. The prime example of this scenario can be seen in the Fleischer Brothers' "Out of the Inkwell" series. Taking one of their earliest works *Tantalizing Fly* (1920) as an example, the film is a culmination of the experimental operation of the interweaving of the flesh-and-blood and the hand-drawn world. It starts with an animator sitting there drawing a cartoon of a clown. A three-dimensional fly (a model) comes to rest on his paper and starts to harass both the animator and the clown. Both of them are irritated. The clown asks for the animator's pen and draws his own "creation" to lure the fly. Their attempts to get the fly are in vain. Exasperated, the clown rips up the paper and hides himself in the crevice. The animator picks up the paper and turns it around to expose the clown, who soon transfers into an ink-drop and slides down the page into the inkwell. The fly follows it into the bottle blindly so that the animator can finally capture the annoying insect. Playing with the division between the cartoon world, which the viewer understood as less "real", and the adjacent photographic world, social satire mixed with reflections on the relationship between the animator, studio and characters. It is not surprising that in the early days the Koko stories involved a struggle for corporeal existence. This strategy of expressing the contest between autonomy and subjection through materiality has been continued in more recent hybrid films such as *La Sexilinea* (Osvaldo Cavandoli 1977) and *Manipulation* (Daniel Greaves 1991). Even in the digital era, the animator's hand is still an effective device with which to fascinate viewers. In 2006 Alan Becker's Flash animation, *Animator vs. Animation,* gained a large number of hits after being posted on the internet. Because of its popularity, the animation prompted two sequels and a game version, and inspired numerous imitations by its viewers, even though it is in many respects simply a retread of those early films – with a drawing desk changed to a computer screen, and the hand changed to the cursor.

Nevertheless, the animator's hand can also be presented metaphorically. In Max Fleisher's "Out of the Inkwell" series, although the main animated character, Koko the Clown, is not directly drawn by the cartoonist, it is always shown as a drop of ink that comes out of the inkwell and falls on the cartoonist's hand. The cartoonist would then blow on the drop, which then instantly turns into a clown. In latter examples such as *You Ought to be in Pictures* (1940) and *Who Framed Roger Rabbit* (1988), the live-action characters are filmmakers, directors, producers or film company bosses. Animated cartoon characters are presented as something being created. Just as those who are displayed alongside an obvious creator's hand, these cartoon figures' destinies are to entertain people, make people laugh, or to follow live-action characters' intentions.

The subordination of the creature to the creator that occurred in the classical narrative of the animator's hand shown in the works above is absent in my practice. The subjectivities of the creator and the creature in my works are both equally constructed, i.e. created with the same degree of artificiality, and equally balanced in the sense of power relationships. For example, in *Nothing to Do with Weather*, the photographic character presented as the creator of the drawn character shows no intention of mastering her creation. In effect, the drawn girl is more an extension than a creation of the photographic one. In order to interact with a drawn background (which is different in kind to a photographic character), the photographic girl gives away a book (representing thought) and a cup of drink (representing energy) when they are passed to the drawn girl. Carrying objects from photographic girl, the drawn girl explores the drawn world on behalf of her creator. In this way, the distinction between the dominant and the dominated is obscure. Unlike that in the classical narrative, there is no innate superiority of the strong over the weak. Retrospectively, there are two possible explanations for this lack of an animator's special power in the practice. The first comes from the conflict of self-consciousness. Although I am the creator of my work, I have had little sense of control in my real life during the course of studying abroad.This conflict might have weakened my own sense of subjectivity and influenced my idea of it as a whole. The other possible explanation is my status as a female. After the film was made, I noticed that being a female might well have predicated my practice; therefore I took a look at animation works by female filmmakers regarding the expression of the relation between the creator and the created. I found that the struggle between the creator and the creature appears less often and is of a less conflictual nature in works by female artists.

Naturally women are the bearers and generators of life but in the early days of film women did not have many opportunities to become animators – another kind of "life giver". Animated filmmaking was a male-dominated profession. In industry women were generally hired only in the lowly role of inkers or painters. Sometimes they might advance to the position of in-betweeners, or an animator's assistants, but rarely worked as animators. The resistance a woman might face if she wished to enter the animation industry can be seen in an example from the 1930s, in a letter that was the response from Walt Disney Productions to a female job seeker: "Women do not do any of the creative work in connection with preparing the cartoons for the screen, as that work is performed entirely by young men. For this reason girls are not considered for the training school. The only work open to women consists of tracing the characters on clear celluloid sheets with India Ink and filling in the tracings on the reverse side with paint according to directions" (Burg 2007). It was probably accepted thinking at that time in the industry that women did not possess the creativity required to be an animator. The very first female animator within the studio system was Lillian Friedman. At the age of nineteen, in 1931 she joined the Fleischer Studios as an in-betweener. In 1933 animator Shamus Culhane recognised her talent and recommended her for advancement to an animator. In his book *Talking Animals and Other People* (1986: 66), Culhane points out that it was not easy for him to convince the other animators to accept a woman working as animator. He had to devise tricks to make her accepted in the all-male environment. Even though Friedman achieved the status of animator she was paid considerably less than her male counterparts. Friedman remained in the job until 1939 when she resigned from Fleischer Studios to be with her family full time.

In terms of independent filmmakers, although a few female filmmakers showed great creativity and innovativeness in the early days, such as the pioneering female animator Lotte Reiniger (1899 - 1981), their achievements were relatively sporadic in the first half of twentieth century. However, in the last quarter of the twentieth century the number of females working as animated filmmakers dramatically increased (Pilling 1992: 5). Yet interestingly, compared to male artists, female artists still present themselves less frequently as the life giver in their works. When they do present themselves in their films as the animator/author/creator, the role portrayed often has different relations with its creation than that portrayed in films made by male artists. In their works, not all the animated figures have to immediately start a rivalry with their creator. Kathy Rose's *Pencil Booklings* (1978) and Joanna Priestley's *Voices* (1985) are two examples. The former begins with the scene when the artist, who resembles Rose and is represented through rotoscoping, paints several characters in the air. The characters soon become lively and talkative, each having a unique personality. They refuse to be characters in Kathy's film and even invite her to join in *their* cartoon. The relation between the artist and its creation appears to be more fluent and relaxed, allowing the created to express their views. Priestley's film uses the artist's physical presence as well as her voice to construct her self-image. As a resemblance of the filmmaker talks to an anthropomorphic mirror, she describes and visualises the fears of aging, gaining weight and wrinkles, as well as things that go bump in the night, monsters of the id, and nuclear holocaust. In the end she concludes that "the attitudes that I hold in my mind create the world that I see", implying that the creation on the screen is the embodiment of her mind, which is basically part of her and inseparable from her.

Using rotoscoping, these two examples are both hybrid works. They reveal the relationship between the animator and the animated through the interface between live action and animation, which is relatively rare in animation works by female artists. In contrast, female artists do not shun issues of sex and gender. Either boldly or humorously, female artists such as Suzan Pitt and Michaela Pavlatova among others express their views with insights into the relationship between the genders. I wondered if this might also arise from gender difference. Perhaps it is the case that for female artists, or the natural life-carrier, creating and being created is not something that troubles their sense of self too much. While male artists are more likely to be obsessed with the relation between the creator and the created, the gender gap often becomes the main source of the subjective struggle for female artists. In this regard, the theme of subjectivity is, as seen in many works by female artists, expressed through a depiction of gender and/or sexuality. From this point of view, I took another look at my earlier works, and found that the subject matter did concern subjectivity – a personal interpretation of the state of being. The most obvious work in this respect is *MENsquito*, a hand-drawn short made in 2003.

MENsquito is a story about man and mosquito. A man is awakened from his sleep by an annoying mosquito. To get away from it, the man runs across the field, dives into the water, and flies high in the sky. He thinks he has escaped the mosquito's persecution. However, the mosquito transforms into a goddess and successfully seduces him. After satisfying the man's dream, it changes back into a giant insect and drinks him up immediately. In this work, the mosquito is the generator of harassment, annoyance, dream and death for the man. I embarked on the creation of this work when my marriage was breaking down. Over a period of three months I relentlessly immersed myself in pencil drawings, resulting in this short film. Although at that time I was depressed and full of remorse for my failed marriage, the female protagonist in the film represented by the mosquito does not have a feeble ego. On the contrary, she appears to be the powerful one in their encounter, revealed by her powers of transformation and cruelty. I think that was due to the sense of control I gained in other aspects of life then. I had a sense of achievement in my profession as a documentary filmmaker. With plenty of resources, I was enjoying the freedom to explore nearly anything I wished, including starting to pursue animated filmmaking. In contrast, the idea of subjectivity presented in the works I made in the UK is much more complex while at the same time more open to compromise than my previous practice. I presumed that there are two possible real-life contexts in which my sense of being weakened contributed to the idea developed after I came to the UK: first, the experience of living abroad; and second, that of being a female. After reviewing *MENsquito*, the only work relating to the issue of subjectivity I made before coming to the UK, I found that being a female does not necessarily predicate a feeble ego in my practice. Therefore, I can speculate that living abroad was the main cause of this sense of weakness, which both instigated my interest in subjectivity and became the main force in shaping its core idea.

As described previously, Ph.D. study can be enormously anxiety-inducing. This practice-led study indeed has been perhaps the most challenging period of my life. The only thing I can count on is my research. However I felt I was making no progress: because of the language, or because I could not grasp what constituted an adequate practice-led research. One year ran into the next. I was stuck in a world where I felt an unwelcome, ineffective and useless foreigner, while on the other side of the earth, my beloved world including my family and my job there started collapsing. A long held desire to become a mother seemed increasingly unlikely. I was stuck in a small room in the UK, feeling barren and frustrated in all my endeavours, yet still having to stay as positive as possible to try to progress the research. Living like this is full of contradictions such as that between self-consciousness and self-forgetfulness. The only possible strategy seemed to become extremely accepting, simply allowing the negative thoughts and feelings to undulate. I gave up controlling them. As for the research, although I did not want to dwell on personal problems, this complexity was inevitably reflected in the practice. I did not realise the role it played in forming my ideas around subjectivity until I finished the films and took a long look at them.

The whole reflection on female consciousness actually demonstrates a kind of relationship between practice and idea. From instinct, animators know that practice is often about challenging or modifying the ideas gathered from prior knowledge. It is similar to my first examination of historical hybrid works in terms of their performance of the relationships between the animator and the animated and the development and application of my own strategy in practice. This way, practice-led research is about making ideas happen. Yet I think another fundamental aspect of practice making is that it is about generating ideas. And for practice-led research, this aspect is perhaps of more importance. Sometimes the initiatives for exploration come from a thought during the practice or a retrospective observation after the practice. I did not think about my identity as a female before I embarked on practice making. When considering the "weak ego" presented in my finished works, I found that my being a female could be a possible factor in my idea of subjectivity. It then led to more contextual review as well as the review of my own early works, and brought me new understandings about the relationship between subjectivity and gender differences. The researcher makes unintentional decisions in the practice, senses them through or after practice making, and then deals with them intellectually, trying to put ideas and experiences together.

Apart from the gender issue, another example of issues emerging from the making of practice is in *Nothing to Do with Weather,* concerning ideas of foreground and background, inside and outside. The sound track indicates that it is rainy outside. The photographic girl has nothing to do but doodle on the drawing pad. Yet although she does not leave the room, a seemingly interior journey kicks off despite the rain. In the last few scenes, a blurring of inside and outside happens when the background is foregrounded. The drawn girl emerges from a trash bin hidden in the background and comes to sit on the sofa in the foreground. The photographic girl then appears behind the window, and collects the cup from the drawn girl in spite of the existence of the window glass. In the process, the distinction between the inside and outside is weakened, making their respective positions reversible and flexible.

Flying Tunes also engages in the operation of inside/outside tension while the play with performance style echoes the play with space. The sense of space is stable at the beginning of the film when the two characters are inside a room or a flat whilst both act in a natural manner. Later, on the balcony, they become more caricatured and "actor-like". A Taiwanese style balcony is integrated into a building rather than protruding from it (fig. 13). Standing on the balcony, the characters are no doubt outside their rooms, but they are also in a place in between the interior and exterior of the apartment. The sense of "somewhere in-between" is further enhanced by the "model-like" appearance of the buildings. Made by 3-D computer software, the buildings are unrealistic in comparison to the live actors, thus appearing similar to models or miniatures (fig. 14). Here we seem to encounter something like a doll's house. The characters are thus reduced to doll-like figures while presenting ordinary emotions in a stagy and theatrical manner (fig. 15). As the inhabitants of doll's house are "uncanny others of those who appear to use it – play with it – in the daytime" (Jervis 2008: 19), the balcony scenes may cast doubt on the "human-ness" of the characters in the viewer's mind. Even though the characters show emotions that might suggest readily identifiable human attributes, which gives them individual identities, they could still provoke a doubt as to whether they might be partly mechanisms that run automatically or are governed by external forces or programming power. It then becomes a performance of selfhood, exhibiting tension between free will and reliance, autonomy and subjection.

Practice-led research is about making ideas happen and also about ideas: ideas before or after practice, ideas generated from or bringing about practice. In a cyclic process (as shown in the Introduction, fig. 0-2) ideas are produced and scrutinised in order to find the ones worth further pursuing. I repeatedly contemplate the array of ideas and sift them by means of writing and practicing. Some ideas are applied to further iterations of practice while some are suspended for the moment. Both gender differences and the inside/outside tension could be associated with the uncanny. It would

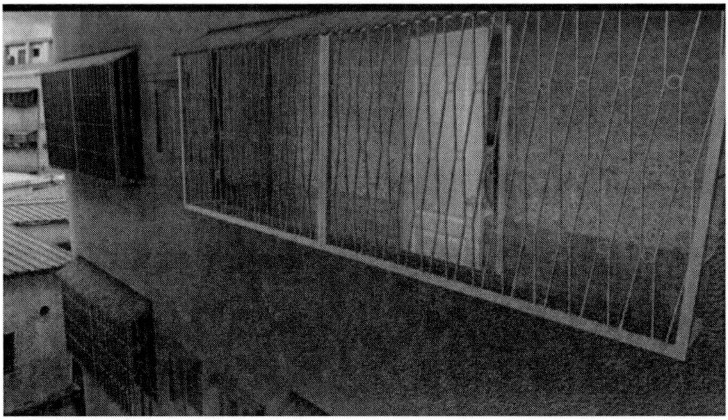

Fig. 13: Taiwanese style balcony is embedded in the surface of a building rather than protruding from it: image from Flying Tunes

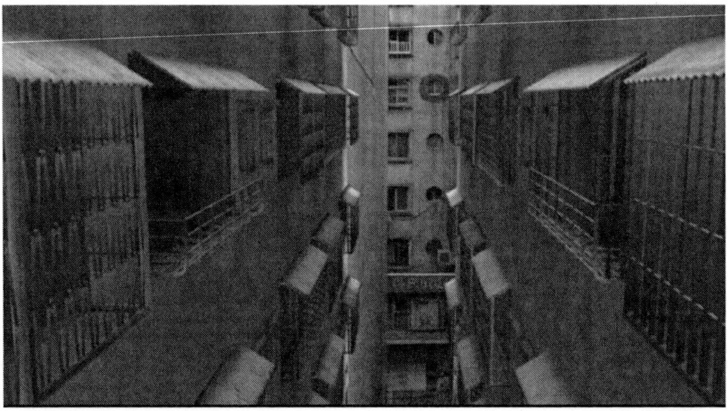

Fig. 14: Made by 3-D computer software, the buildings look a little unrealistic: image from Flying Tunes

be interesting to further consider the links between them and find something that can be tested in further practice. However, there are other ideas and observations that require consideration. Regarding the theme of subjectivity, I have talked about my personal subjective consciousness, how it influenced the idea of subjectivity presented in my practice, and gender as a possible factor. Next I am going to focus more on the identity of an animated filmmaker, a very fundamental part in the struggle between the animator and the animated.

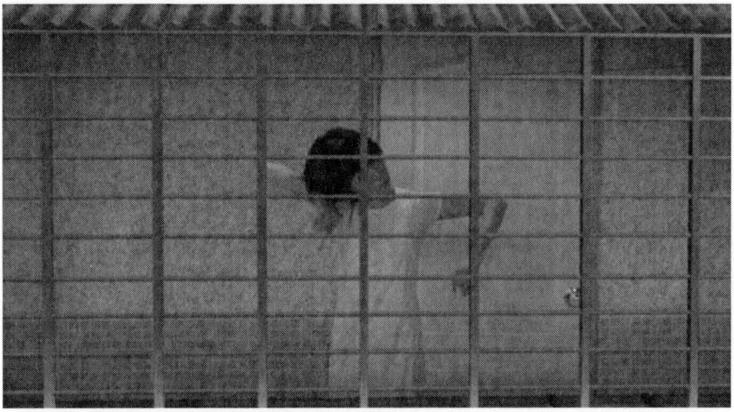

Fig. 15: The character at the balcony is reduced to the doll-like while performing in a stagey manner: image from Flying Tunes

3.3 Representation of Filmmaking Practice and Creative Subjectivity

Animating Animator the Animated is about an animator and her work. It shows the animator drawing against a light box, flicking over drawings to check their consistency, and then watching them moving on a TV screen. This short film is a kind of self-portrait illustrating the animator at work. The seemingly simple work actually represents a time-consuming technical process, and therefore asks questions about animated films' capacity for self-reflexiveness – the difference between the representation of filmmaking and the real filmmaking process.

The self-portrait of the author can lead us to the question of the representation of artistic practice which is often associated with the representation of an artist's identity and tools. There is a long history of individuals being portrayed in paintings by showing specific tools or clothing related to their profession. These objects are visual attributes of the portrayed person. For example, a celestial globe as the symbol for an astronomer in the Durer astronomer by Albrecht Dürer in 1504 (fig. 3-3), a set of measuring instruments for a mathematician in *Nicholas Kratzer*by Hans Holbein in 1528, and a nautical map for a geographer in *The Geographer* by Johannes Vermeer, c. 1668-69. Artists have also represented their practice or professional identity by displaying attributes of painting in their own works. Some of the first representations of artists at work may be found in illuminated manuscripts and in the early Renaissance where we find St. Luke painting the Madonna as a way to depict artistic practice and skill (Lehmann 2009: 33). During the Renaissance the iconography of artistic practice evolved into the self-portrait of the artists who often appeared in the act of painting themselves at the easel with their workshop as the background (Lehmann 2009: 33; Hernandez 2010: 42).

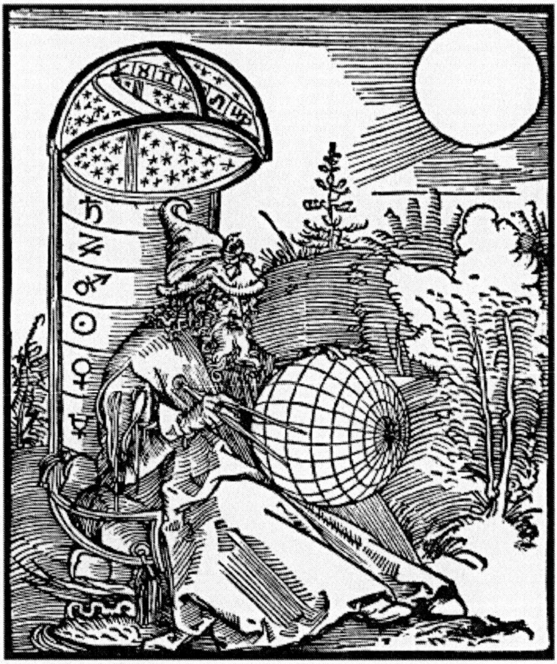

Fig. 3-3: Durer astronomer, an engraving of an astronomer by Albrecht Dürer, from the title page of Messahalah, De scientiamotusorbis*, 1504*
(Source: Grand Lodge of British Columbia and Yukon*,*
http://freemasonry.bcy.ca/art/astronomer.html)

Despite the variety of techniques and changing technologies, the iconography of "the artist at work" is still common in modern times. In the case of animated filmmaking, early animators tended to interject themselves into their films. The way they presented themselves was a direct adaptation of classical iconography. For example, in J. Stuart Blackton's *The Echanted Drawing* (1900), *Humorous Phases of Funny Faces* (1906) and *Lighting Sketches* (1907), the artist is shown as an illustrator or lighting sketch artist at his easel, creating drawings which are animated then in the film. However, the self-portrait that drew attention to the processes and procedures of animation filmmaking did not appear until Winsor McCay's films.

People today may have difficulty imagine how the frame-by-frame technique could seem like magic. However, in the earliest days, part of the attraction of animated films came from the secret of the trick effects that animators were eager to conceal. Although self-figuration was often a characteristic of early animated films, animators before Winsor McCay usually portrayed themselves (directly or by implication) as a kind of sorcerer or magician. Film companies also used a sense of mystery to market animated films. In the discussion of *The Haunted Hotel*, the animated film created in 1907 using stop-frame technique that aroused enormous public curiosity at that time, Crafton (1982: 16-18) elaborates on how the public aura of mystery and insolubility was deliberately built around animated films in the first decade of twentieth century. As the mystery of animated films needed to be sustained, the image of the animator tended to be someone who was able to do mysterious things. McCay, however, did not continue this image. From his very first film, he portrayed himself as something else.

Before setting foot in animated motion pictures, McCay was an artist-reporter and newspaper cartoonist. He also performed "chalk talk"in vaudeville. In 1911 McCay completed his first animated film. It was based on his "Little Nemo" comic strip, and was intended to be presented in a vaudeville show. The film started with a live-action prologue followed byhand-drawn animation. There has been debate about whether a short all-animated version was completed and used on the vaudeville stage before the release of the motion-picture version. According to Crafton (1982: 98-100), when the idea was being presented for the first time on the stage, it already had the prologue that accompanies the film as we see today. The prologue is a self-portrayal of the author and a tale of challenge. Explaining the origin and process of the animated work, it shows the versatility and skilfulness of the animator. In the prologue, McCay is in company with several friends at a club. He tells them his new idea for a cartoon. In this scene, close-up shots focus on McCay rapidly drawing the four characters for the animated cartoon, which is an exhibition of his skill of caricaturing. The artist then makes a bet with his sceptical friends and signs a contract, agreeing to turn out 4,000 pictures in one month's time for a moving picture company. In the following scenes McCay demonstrates his perseverance working at his studio. With hundreds of drawings piled on his desk, McCay seems absorbed by his labour. Meanwhile, workers keep entering carrying tons of paper and ink barrels. These comical scenes underline the effort required in the production of animation, which is now an iconic image of animation production. Another iconographic element of animated filmmaking seems to be the presence of technological elements. The scene in which McCay's young assistant attempts to flip the drawings on the Mutoscope, a rotating drum for testing the consistency of drawings, is useful for the iconography of animation as a novelty and of the animator as a resourceful technician. In this film, McCay was already portraying himself as a craftsman or technician, rather than magician.

This self-portrayal device continues throughout most of McCay's subsequent works. His animated films often begin with a live-action prologue, explaining the circumstances where the "artist McCay" undertakes this task, along with the exhibition of his studio and the animation equipment. Usually the prologue contains a bet or a mission which indicates the amount of pictures needed to make the film. The "bet" also plays a crucial role in modelling the profession of an animator. The numbers increase for every new work, showing that every task is more difficult than the previous one, and the achievement of the animator becomes greater each time. Crafton (1982: 129) discusses the attitude disclosed by the insertion of these live-action prologues:

> Repeatedly we are told, in the advertising and in the films themselves, about the thousands of drawings and the hours of labor required for each cartoon. It is this affinity for revealing the means of production that distinguishes McCay from the first generation of trickfilm artists. Méliès, Booth, and Blackton were adamant in refusing to divulge the secrets of animation – an attitude completely alien to McCay. Rather than figuring himself as a nineteenth-century stage magician, McCay represents himself as a modern technician.

Through those prologues, McCay tells the audience that all the magical, wonderful images were the product of the rational and technology. By revealing the apparatus and the process, he lets the audience understand that even a short animation demands thousands or even tens of thousands of drawings and amazingly skilled labour, giving the animator a different identity from the magician.

Although caricatured, the prologue to the "Little Nemo" animation is basically true to the reality of the development of animation production. Could this be the first time the animation process was presented? It seems that McCay was interested in dispelling the magical aura of images on the screen. However what he had done might just be the opposite. He chose to evade the question of how his drawings were put together to create the fantastical "moving images". Usually in his films the crucial part of the *bringing to life* tricks, namely the shooting and editing of drawings, is concealed, remaining in the "black box" (Crafton 1982: 16-18; Hebert 2005: 183), a term used to refer to technical secrets/skills hidden and accessible only to those with such skills. The audience always sees the resultant film directly without witnessing how the frames are recorded and processed. The mystery of animated filmmaking therefore increases through this revealing-and-concealing strategy. In effect the "Little Nemo" film functioned as a promotional vehicle for the multi-talented Winsor McCay. This is quite obvious from the film's title: *Winsor McCay, the Famous Cartoonist of the N.Y. Herald and His Moving Comics*. In this sense McCay's hybrid films may be regarded as the predecessor of today's "Making-Of", or behind the scene, genre. In a contemporary "Making-Of", artistic practice is also displayed without giving away the secret of the actual how-to. Regardless of their promise to reveal the making-of illusion, key elements of its magic are deliberately withheld. Through a selective representation of animation and CGI making process, the audience learns that a huge amount of work and skill is required in the creation of illusionist imagery. The ability of its makers is more admired, and the fascination of the final product increases. At the end the "Making-Of" is more about advertising a coming attraction than it is about technical enlightenment.

The "Making-Of" shows the distance between representations of digital filmmaking and the actual process. Yet does it also remind us just how difficult it would be to reveal and represent the digital filmmaking process? Lehmann (2009: 34) argues that digital modes of production do not appear to favour the representation of the actual process; one of the factors is that the metaphor of the artist's workplace has changed; it is "frequently referred to as a laboratory rather than a studio or atelier". Using the iconography of the laboratory may just be an element for obscuring the making process of digital cinema. The laboratory, in the sphere of science, has been described as "a place where experiment and invention are kept from public view, and only finite results are allowed to emerge after having been carefully wrapped in impenetrable layers of scientific reasoning" (Lehmann 2009: 35). The idea of "artist's laboratory", therefore, may carry the laboratory's tradition of not describing the mess behind the walls of the labs.

The notion of experiment and laboratory is appealing. It is always possible to make an ambiguous process look like it is completely planned. However, for creativity it is often serendipity and surprises during the process that plays a vital role in its development. To report and reflect on a filmmaking process as though it is a well-planned experiment would be far from the reality and have little reference value for further experiment.

Another difficulty in representing the filmmaking process may come from its incorporation of the use of digital technology. It is not easy to represent artistic practice in the digital era when much of the core experiment happens inside the computer. How do we describe and visualise the procedures of data programming and processing? The employment of modern technologies not only brings difficulty to the self-revelation aspects of animated filmmaking, it also imbues animated filmmaking with a quality of uncanniness. Many early animated films seem to exhibit this sense of the uncanny. Many of the tricks, from phantasmagoria shows to early film and beyond, are associated with a sense of the uncanny by rendering an ordinary world extraordinary. The processes that are kept opaque to non-initiates have been described by scholars and filmmakers as "black box", a term that can refer to anything that has mysterious or unknown internal functions or mechanisms (*Merriam-Webster* on-line dictionary). With better and better user-friendly interfaces, advanced technologies seem to make the filmmaking process easier, or at least more accessible. Computers are ordinary machines that we can manipulate relatively easily. However, they are also machines few of us understand completely – or even partly. Relying more and more on digital technologies, contemporary animated filmmaking inevitably carries a sense of the uncanny caused by an experience that exceeds our reflexive grasp (Jervis 2008: 28-29).

I often have a strange feeling when I am creating CGI effects. When I make a nice fire effect with just a few clicks, who is the creator of the fire? Is it me, the computer or the person who designed the software? In *Animating Animator the Animated*, the animator collects all the drawing papers, and stuffs them into a TV set. Like a magic box, the TV soon turns the drawings into a moving figure dancing on the screen. It is as if the life is given by the electronic TV rather than the animator. Computers and other advanced electronic devices have helped modern people, including contemporary filmmakers, to carry out complicated work effortlessly. However, as discussed above, the technologies are actually virtual black boxes with concealed mechanisms and tricks that are beyond most people's understanding. Sometimes I wonder if they are living things that can in some way govern my life. Contemporary filmmakers have a dependence on technology. However, unlike most applied scientists who heavily rely on the expensive and complicated equipment to perform experiments in their laboratory, independent filmmakers can access or possess digital tools much more easily. Filmmakers tend to forget their dependence on the technology, and therefore digital tools are more likely to crawl into the dark corner of a filmmaker's eyes, bringing a sense of uncanniness into the process of filmmaking.

The uncanniness of technology is used here to indicate a sense of the unknown, an uncertainty that fills the individual with perplexity. In the practice I tried to add this kind of uncertainty into the description of the collective assemblage of individuals. In the last scenes of *Flying Tunes*, there is a lady in a Victorian outfit playing the Thaumatrope (fig. 3-4). The Victorian era of British history covered more than half of the nineteenth century. It was the era of the birth and popularity of optical toys such as the Thaumatrope as well as condensed spectacles such as a doll's house.

This lady thus has implications for social and cultural contexts. Within some scenes the male and the female protagonists act as if they are under the spell of the fly (fig. 3-5). But when the fly comes to settle on the lady's finger, she seems to be the master of the fly (fig. 3-6). The superior-subordinate relationship becomes somewhat uncertain when considering another work: in *Animating Animator the Animated* it is implied that the real master/animator is the spider, a small and unnoticeable insect that represents the invisible forces of nature (fig. 3-7). The insect in *Animating Animator the Animated* is hinted to be the master, the one who animates everything in the film including the animator/author, while the insect in *Flying Tunes* is just a minuscule messenger of the lady. Alternatively, if the lady represents the power of social and cultural contexts, she herself is just the product of the assemblage. It then becomes a multiplicity of relationships in which the status and significance of any being appears to be diminished.

In general, the "master behind master" or "master within master" story simply indicates the non-existence of real autonomy. Such a view, appearing to privilege the connectivity of an assemblage over the identity of its constituent individual parts may become a submissive subjectivity in partriarchal systems such as Confucianism in Chinese culture. However, the emphasis on uncertainty makes it a totally different kind of subjectivity, which is expressed by Taoism.

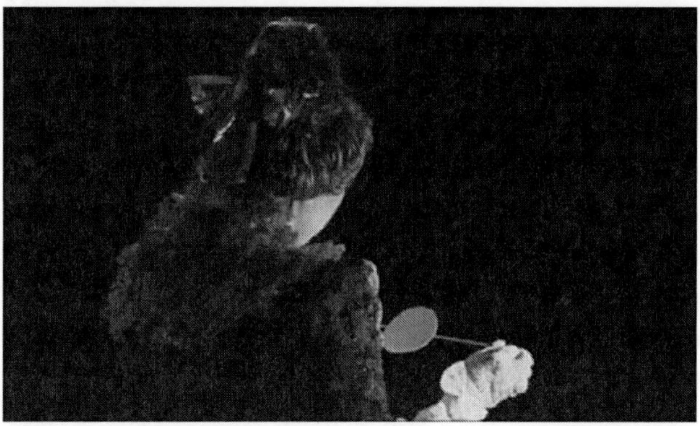

Fig. 3-4: The lady in Victorian outfit playing the thaumatrope: image from Flying Tunes

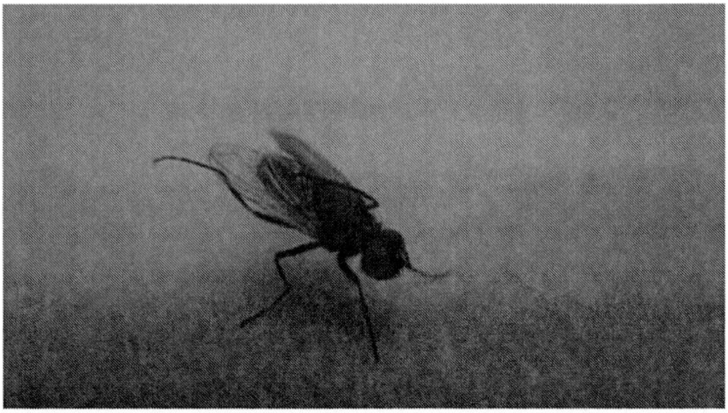

Fig. 3-5: The insect in Flying Tunes

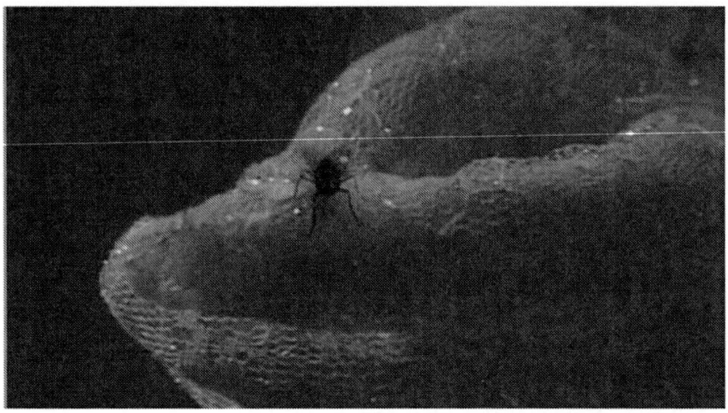

Fig. 3-6: The insect rests on the finger of the lady in Victorian costume: image from Flying Tunes

Because of its preference for single authority figures, for thousands of years Chinese rulers chose Confucianism as their legitimating philosophy. Confucianism was so influential that not only the Chinese, but "many Asian cultures have distinct conceptions of individuality that insists on the fundamental relatedness of individuals to each other" (Markus &Kitayama 1991: 24). Influenced by Chinese Confucianism, the concepts of selfhood in many Asian countries are relation-centred, not individual-centred as in the West (Huang 2011). Confucianism stresses the individual's embeddedness in the social network. The life of the individual is incomplete; it derives meaning only from the coexistence of other individuals (Ho 1995). While they do demand selfhood to be reciprocal and malleable, Confucians do not advocate a dissolution of the self/non-self-boundary; as a mutable self is not acknowledged by Confucius. However in a multiplicity of relationships where uncertainty is emphasised and respected, the self-other demarcation will be called into question. And this can only be achieved by other philosophical traditions such as Taoism.

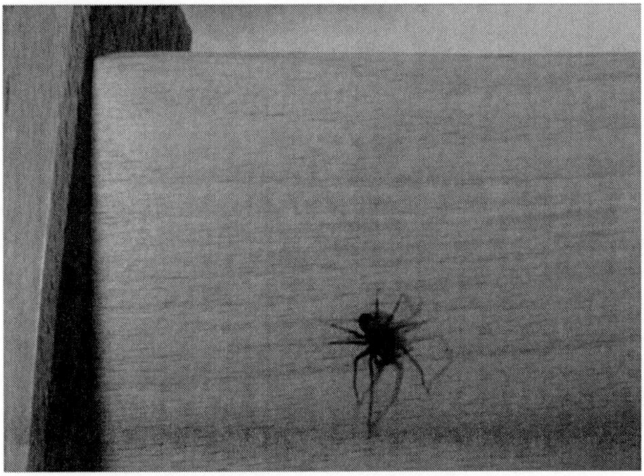

Fig. 3-7: The insect in Animating Animator the Animated

Indigenous to China, Taoism may represent the Chinese counterculture. Taoists disdain the Confucian adherence to social convention, hierarchical organisation and governmental rule by the scholar class (Ho 1995). Their views on demarcation and distinction are shown in *Tao Te Ching*, a fundamental Taoist text written around the 6th century BC. The following text is an example:

> When everyone in the world knows the beautiful as beautiful, ugliness comes into being.
> When everyone knows the good, then the not good comes to be.
> The mutual production of being and nonbeing,
> The mutual completion of difficult and easy,
> The mutual formation of long and short,
> The mutual filling of high and low,
> The mutual harmony of tone and voice,
> The mutual following of front and back –
> These are all constants.
> Therefore the Sage dwells in nonactive affairs and practices the wordless teaching.
> The ten thousand things arise, but he doesn't begin them;
> He acts on their behalf, but he doesn't make them dependent;
> He accomplishes his tasks, but he doesn't dwell on them;

> It is only because he doesn't dwell on them that they therefore do not leave him.
> (*Tao Te Ching*, Chapter 2, translated by Henricks 1993: chapter 2)

According to the above, to consider something as ugly, one needs the concept of beauty. If you have hatred for a particular colour, that is simply because you have love for some other colour first. The discrimination is constructed, and your hatred toward something has nothing to do with its essence. This attitude is totally different from Confucianism, especially considering Confucius's comment on purple mentioned in Chapter 2.

The Taoist self is without a centre and is not hierarchically organised. The Taoist conception of self is like a deconstructed Western self. It has often been compared with Derrida's deconstructionism. Derrida's deconstructed self is decentred and multidimensional. Selfhood contains both other-in-self and self-in-other, rather than being an entity set contrastively against other entities (Sampson 1989). Derrida's deconstruction comes from the endeavour to deconstruct the Western tradition, using intellectual tools coming from that very tradition. The concept of dichotomy is fundamental in its methodology while both the tool and the target waited to be deconstructed. From a Taoist stance, however, to frame the question about the self in terms of subject-object dichotomy would lead nowhere, since Chuang-tzu proclaims that "the great Tao is all-embracing without making distinctions" (Ho 1995). This statement eliminates both construction and deconstruction. Yet how could one possibly know what a deconstructed deconstructionism is like? Taoism itself is the embodiment of paradoxes. The only way to grasp its spirit is perhaps to ponder on those fantastic Taoist fables told by Taoist philosophers. Regarding the notion of "mastering and being mastered", I would like to mention a story told by Chuang-tzu, which is a conversation between shadow and the shadow's shadow, the penumbra (wangliang 罔兩):

> Penumbra asked Shadow, "In the past you were walking, but now you stop. In the past you were sitting, but now you get up. Why is there no fixity and independence in your activities?" Shadow replied, "Am I like this because I have something to wait for and depend upon? Is what I wait for and depend upon like this also, since it, too, has something to wait for and depend upon? Is my waiting and dependence like that of a snake upon his skin or a cicada upon his wings — or is it not? How would I ever know the reasons for what is and is not the case?"(Translated by Nylan 2008: 127).

Shadow is here scolded by its shadow, the penumbra, as lacking in independence and a true self. It wisely responds with a query that questions a single true corporeal self of any object, person or thing, as well as the independence of the subjective experience of self. Being a story told thousand years ago, it could, in my opinion, in effect illustrate the contemporary idea of the author as "the product of a period, of a class, of a gender, of aspirations that are socially determined" (Hernandez 2010: 46).

The creative self is not distinct or in opposition to its creation. I tried to address such a decentred subjectivity in my practice through the exploration of hybrid techniques. I presented myself, the author, as an animated character in two films (*Nothing to Do with Weather* and *Animating Animator the Animated*). The self-portrait of the author as animated figure through stop-frame photography and pixilation technique constitutes "doppelganger" (Freud 2009: 41) that may steal authority, autonomy and authenticity from the author, transforming him/her into a "fictional author" that is alienated from the real author. It may disturb the relationships between animated characters, fictional authors and the real author, making the creative subjectivity a product of uncertainty. The creation of the hybridised character has a vital role in my exploration of notions of self-in-other and other-in-self. Therefore in the next section I will discuss the formation and function of hybridised character.

3.4 Hybridised Character and Estranged Subjectivity

There are two main ways to create hybridised characters. The first is by integrating heterogeneous movement and figuration; and the second is by putting heterogeneous parts into the same figure. I would call these two ways, *hybridisation within the character* and *hybridisation upon the character*. *Hybridisation within the character* means animating a photographic figure (e.g. pixilated figure), or the integration of a hand-drawn or CGI figure with conventional live-action movement (e.g. figures made by rotoscoping and motion capture). When the figure is seen as a still image (i.e. taken from the film) the viewer cannot tell it is a hybridised figure, but when it moves it becomes clear that it is. *Hybridisation upon the character* means the appearance of the figure derives from heterogeneous elements, but the movement is not a concern, for example, the protagonists in the *Angry Kid* series (1999 - present), *City Paradise* (2004), and *Madame Tutli-Putli* (2008). Before the digital era, hybridised characters could only be achieved through a limited set of approaches. The level of difficulty in production was higher compared with a non-hybridised character. As pointed out by Manovich (2002: 157), computer technology privileges spatial dimensions that were not available to be exploited in the pre-digital time. The use of digital technology opens new possibilities for the production of hybridised characters because it makes it easier. The approaches are now many and various. Yet, just as in the pre-digital era, they remain two distinct kinds of hybridisation.

However, these two kinds of hybridisation could be combined, mixed together. I demonstrate mixed hybridisationin *Flying Tunes*. In the final scenes, the characters are integrated with digitally manipulated movement. Moreover, some of their parts are replaced by computer animation to enhance their cartooniness. In this sense, the hybridised figures are the assemblage of the two kinds of hybridisation. As the hybridised figures are intentionally employed in the practice, the discussion in this section will proceed from the effects of the two kinds of hybridised characters, to the functions of technology in producing hybridisations, and then the meaning of the hybridised subjectivity in our age.

The first type of hybridisation – hybridisation within the character – often causes confusion about the character's material or existential identity. Techniques include old-style rotoscoping, pixilation and, in contemporary digital cinema, motion capture. The blending of heterogeneous movement and figuration into one character raises issues of life as representation, and the self as constructed. Its operation could be discussed from various viewpoints. For example, in *I move, so I am* (Gerrit van Dijk 1998), the author uses rotoscoping to create a self-representation that expresses the animator's identity figuratively. The film starts with a hand drawing the other hand, and then the shoulders, head, legs and the animator himself. The figure of the animator then engages in constant actions of animating things and reinventing himself. Presented in restless, continual motion, the hybridised figure reveals the construction of the acting self. Appearing to be an adaptation of Descartes "I think, so I am", the title "I move, so I am" seems concerned with the interdependence between the body and the brain. Yet the employment of rotoscoping also implies the non-integration of one's subjectivity. The technique I explored was pixilation rather than rotoscoping, but the non-integration of subjectivity is what interested me. Explicit in the works or not, I actually found a non-integration through the production process.

In *Animating Animator the Animated* there are two kinds of pixilation: one can be seen in the dancing clip on the TV screen (fig. 3-8), and the other in the last scene in the kitchen (fig. 3-9). While the kitchen scene is a normal pixilation, the production process for the dancing clip is more complicated. A hand-drawn animation was made in advance as the reference for the performance of the live actor that is myself. During the shooting, stop-motion software was used to check whether my postures tallied with the drawings. As I could not reach the computer and check the tracing paper while I was performing the poses, someone had to be there to give me spoken instructions and even come over to adjust my position as if I was a puppet. Although it was I who designed the movement and made the drawings, guided by stop-motion software and the assistants[9], I had no idea what would be the next position for posing and shooting. I was deprived of normal feedback about the position of my body, and could only keep track of it through the assistant's judgement. In addition, for each frame, I had to concentrate on controlling my body and holding it in one position for a while. The feelings of being lost and concentrating on controlling my body at the same time was both intriguing and disturbing. I was controlling my body but it felt out of my control; I raised my leg, but the pose felt alien. I did not know if this sense of non-integration was observable in the resultant film. It did make the animated movement jiggle, which was not exactly what I intended. I therefore tried a new kind of pixilation experiment, which can be seen in *Flying Tunes*, a work finished after *Animating Animator the Animated*, with the concept and process delineated in Chapter 4.

Apart from integrating heterogeneous movement and figuration, there is obviously another way to create hybridised character: hybridisation upon the character, namely to put heterogeneous parts into the same body. In Hollywood mainstream films these parts are often adjusted into the same visual style and combined seamlessly. Even so, interesting questions may be asked on the strength of the advanced compositing technology. Films raise philosophical questions, such as *Repo Men* (2010) which could be said to ask "What makes me ME?". In this futuristic action-thriller, humans have extended and improved lives through indestructible mechanical organs provided by advanced technology. Imagine I have a bicycle. When the tyres are worn I replace them. When the frame breaks I replace it. After a while I replace everything on this bicycle. Is it still my bicycle? Similarly, if I extend my life by replacing broken parts of my body until most parts are replaced, is it still me? How many organs should be left to keep me the same person? Has my identity changed after I have had my heart or brain replaced? Are there any defining organs? What is the minimal sense of self? By crossing the boundaries between machine and human, not only the boundaries between life and death but also those between the self and non-self are broken or disturbed.

[9] The process required at least two assistants, with one to monitor the computer and give instruction and the other to adjust the live actor's positions.

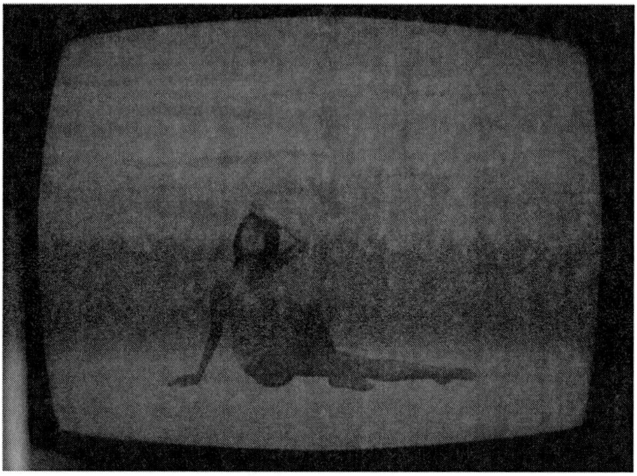

Fig. 3-8: In Animating Animator the Animated, *the dancing clip on the TV screen is made by pixilation via a complicated process*

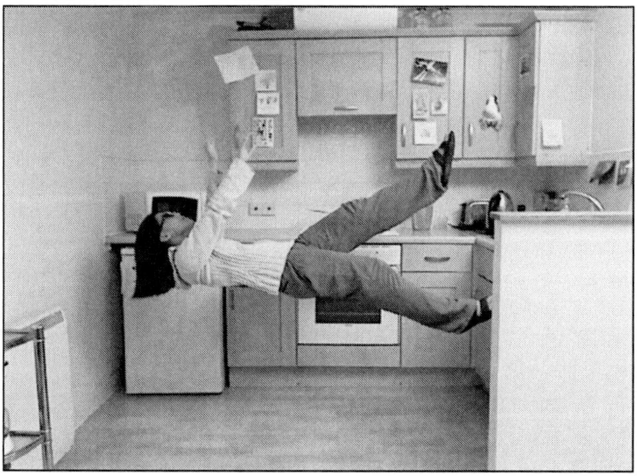

Fig. 3-9: In Animating Animator the Animated, *the last scene in the kitchen is made by normal pixilation*

In the case of experimental films or shorts, the traces of heterogeneity are often retained or even emphasised. In the live-action/ animated hybrid film *City Paradise* (Gaelle Denis 2004), the protagonist's head is live action while the body is made by computer and hand-drawn animation. The slender and distorted animation limbs are especially suitable for depicting the desolation of life in the metropolis. When, later, the protagonist discovers the mysterious, colourful underground world below the metropolis, the caricaturised body also suits the fairy-tale like atmosphere well.

As indicated by Manovich (2001: 143), digital compositing presents a strong sense of anti-montage aesthetics in which the combination of heterogeneous elements is emphatically *not* intended to establish contrast, complementarity or dissonance between them. This is consistent with the world characterised by culture theorists as a world of hyperreality. According to Baudrillard (1983: 2), we are living in a world where simulated feelings and experiences have replaced the real thing: "It is the generation by models of a real without origins or reality: a hyperreal." In *Travels in Hyperreality*(1986: 8) Umberto Eco refers to "the absolute fake" and defines it as "a form of hyperreality in which a cultural artefact is perceived as an improved copy, more "real" than its original". Paul Virilio (1991: 34) has also discussed a similar process in which our world and our lives have effectively become "cinematised" or "mediatised", and our sense of reality increasingly becomes confused with a pervasive "reality effect". As Telotte (2010: 7) points out, instead of suggesting that the real has simply disappeared and been replaced by simulacra, Virilio wants to call attention to "how we have increasingly allowed that "reality effect" to stand in for the real". For live-action/animated hybrids, the dominant aesthetic featuring photorealistic, seamless compositing, and harmonised fantastic realism simply reflects how we mix fear with desire and the attempts to secure ourselves in an illusive world. In a world described by Fredric Jameson as characterised by the "decentring of that formerly centered subject or psyche" (Jameson 1991: 14-15) and the "waning of affect", where feelings are "free-floating and impersonal and tend to be dominated by a peculiar kind of euphoria" (ibid.: 64), how does a filmmaker respond to it through the integration of live action and animation?

City Paradise by Gaelle Denis mentioned above could be an example of this. Another is Chris Lavis's and MaciekSzczerbowski's *Madame Tutli-Putli*. As described in Chapter 1, it combines real human eyes on the faces of stop motion puppets. It uses the confrontation of live action and animation as an artistic device to create an effect that I call derealisation. As discussed in Chapter 2, if hyperrealisation is an effect to make people feel the cinematic/fictional world is more real than reality, then derealisation, in contrast, shifts the focus to the feeling of unreality. Maybe the peculiar effect of the simulacrum of hyperreality actually lies in the derealisation of the whole surrounding world of everyday life. The film simply signifies a possibility to reflect on this very hyperrealised subjectivity.

"The Fuccons", a Japanese TV comedy series, may be another, more radical example. Featuring a family of Americans (the Fuccons) living in metropolitan Japan, the series is notable in that all of the characters are played by mannequins with perpetually frozen postures and facial expressions. The fact that the audience could totally understand the story, and could automatically interpret those frozen postures into movements and performances that are required for the story, demonstrates the significance of the viewer's function in the realisation of a film work. For an audience willing to engage in the narrative, the motionless lips may appear to be perfectly in sync with the dialogue. In its use of mannequins, "The Fuccons" reminds us of the uncanniness of the human-thing engagement. The only scene in the whole series that is animated is when Micky, the Fuccons' little boy, imagines that he is an ingenious dancer and dances so vividly and nimbly that it becomes even weirder in its effect than all the uncanny mannequin stills. Marx (1990: 165) claims that commodities become "autonomous figures endowed with a life of their own". As a result, we can become thing-like while living under forces that are "figured" by things. The existence of "The Fuccons" series also seems to imply that this hyperrealised world needs something extra, a more radical element, to produce any sense of shock. It could be argued that such absurdity is a form of continuation or even an elaboration of hyperrealism. Yet in a sense the absurdity actually renews the hyperrealist impetus by asking certain questions about the operations of the illusion of movement, performance and montage on the construction of moving images, aside from the human-thing issue in the contemporary era.

In summary, subjectivity has been an effective theme explored by hybrid films. Hybrid works are now everywhere, not only in Hollywood blockbusters, but also in works by independent filmmakers and multimedia artists, who are enthusiastic about using digital technology to integrate different elements in a video. Putting multi-source elements together is a primary tendency in the so-called "postmodern culture". Yet, do we integrate live-action footage with animation only because it is so easy and common now? How can we make it work in a postmodernist context? The answer lies in how we see the interface between live action and animation as an artistic device. This chapter argues that one issue the interface between live action and animation prioritises is that of subjectivity. In this digital era, a hyperrealised subjectivity is something filmmakers can reconfigure and represent reflexively through the power of digital technologies.

As previously observed, pursuing Ph.D. study abroad can turn out to involve a long period of uncertainty, and feeling oneself in a state of suspension could seem to become a way of life. What I have realised is that what I learned most through this process is not filmmaking; and it is not writing the thesis nor doing research – what I have learned most during these years is about adjusting one's self, about being willing to live with anxiety and to make the best of it. As I considered the frustrating sense of not achieving anything during the study, I re-discovered some interesting foundations for my experience in Taoist non-duality. Although I borrowed ideas from Taoist stories, this research is far from an exploration of Taoist philosophy since it begins from and is based on the "difference" of things – the difference and tension between live action and animation. For Taoists, this concept of discrimination is simply unreal. However for a totally Western concept of "research" that embraces intellectual and progressive attitudes, even though we can try to deconstruct discrimination, it is not feasible to leave it behind. Therefore, in the next chapter, the last part of this thesis, I will go back to "Western style discrimination" to discuss the difference between the condensation and dissection of time.

CHAPTER FOUR

POSES AND MOVEMENT

Anyone who is currently studying animation would have learned the golden principles for cartoon's realistic effect developed by the leading Disney animators and other Hollywood followers from the 1930s onwards. With the first formal introduction made by Disney animators Ollie Johnston and Frank Thomas in their 1981 book entitled *Illusion of Life: Disney Animation*, the famous "twelve principles" aimed to produce an illusion of life-like characters adhering to the basic laws of physics for greater realism in animation. For example, the principle of "slow in and slow out", by giving more frames near the beginning and the end of a movement and fewer in the middle, suggests animators imitate the acceleration and slowing down of real movement. The principle of "arcs" advises animators to always reproduce animated movement in arcs since most human and animal actions occur along an arched trajectory. Other principles such as "squash and stretch", "anticipation", "follow through and overlapping action" and "secondary action" all have been used to serve the realist purpose. Although this set of principles is most fully realised in hand-drawn animation, it has been widely used by non-drawn animation to achieve the "cartooniness" of hand-drawn animation or to enhance a sense of realism to prevent the animated figures from looking like automatons. It is also pertinent to the study of digital cinema. With a little modification, this set of principles could work in all kinds of animation for greater naturalistic outcomes. However, the technique of pixilation has rarely demonstrated cartoon's realist effect in spite of its kinship with the animation family. It has mostly been used to create surreal effects, as seen in many masterpieces such as Raoul Servais's *Harpa* (1978) and the Bolex Brothers' *The Secret Adventures of Tom Thumb* (1993).

Being an investigation focusing on the interface between live action and animation, one of my research efforts has been to experiment with the integration of pixilation and cartoon principles. The results appear in two places: one is in *Animating Animator the Animated*: after the spider steps on the remote, a photographic moving figure appears on the TV screen (time code: 01'48" - 02'05"); the other is in the final part of *Flying Tunes*, when the boy and the girl return to their rooms and start trying to swipe at the fly (time code: 06'42" - 07'58"). They are the results of two very different integrating methods, with the second method a revision and an improvement of the first.

The first method is quite straightforward: first design and make the hand-drawn animation (fig. 3-1); second, scan the drawings and import them into stop motion software; connect computer with shooting device; third, capture the actor's image (in front of green screen) into computer; forth, make the actor pose just like each drawing (with the guidance of the stop-motion software) and then shoot, frame by frame (fig. 3-2); and finally put all the photographs together and the result is the pixilation footage.

I planned to make the pixilation footage as smooth as the drawn animation. However the result was contrary to my expectations. As described in Chapter 3, pixilation made in this way was even more jiggly than that made without drawn references. I thought the problem might come from the fluidity of my drawn animation or the inability to control my body (I was the performer for this part). Therefore I turned to traditional cartoon clips and professional actors (fig. 3-3, 3-4), making them act out the movement of the cartoon clips using exactly the same method. Yet the result was still not convincing, and certainly did not feel like a cartoon at all.

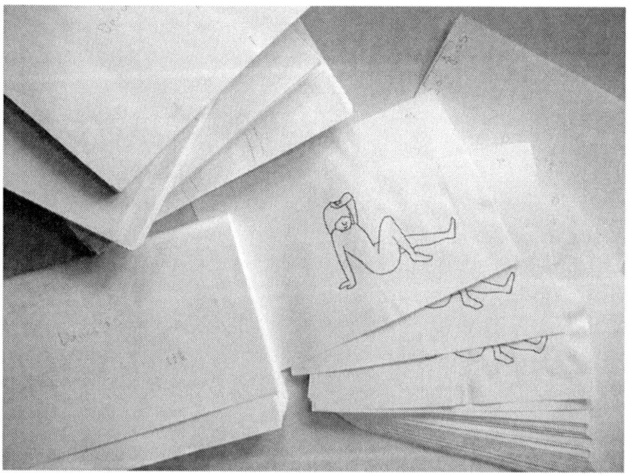

Fig. 3-1: Hand-drawn animation

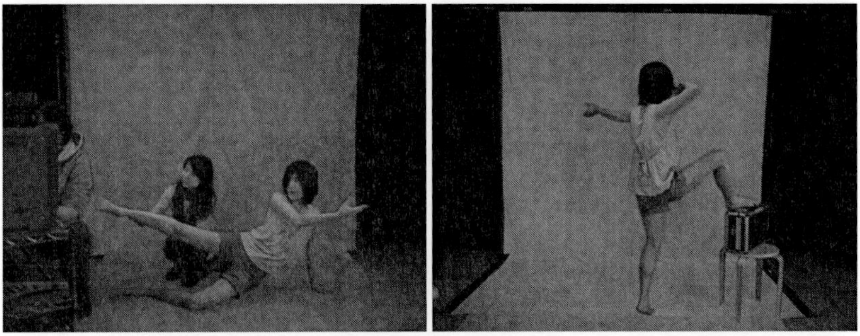

Fig. 3-2: Using a chair or other support to maintain the actor's posture as each capture needs 5-10 seconds to be completed. (In this case the actor is the author herself).

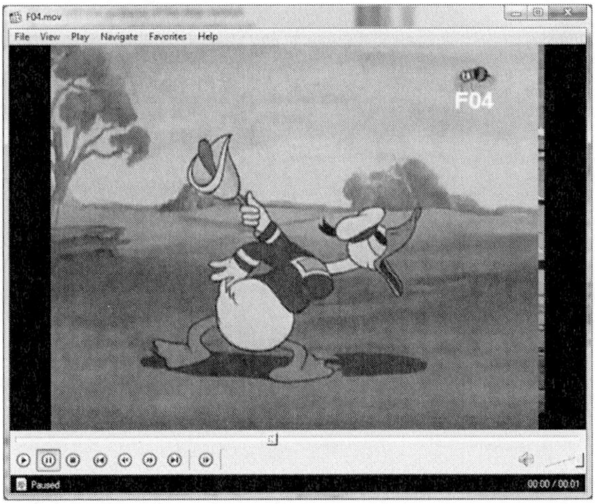

Fig. 3-3: Using traditional cartoon clips as reference to conduct the actor's performance frame by frame

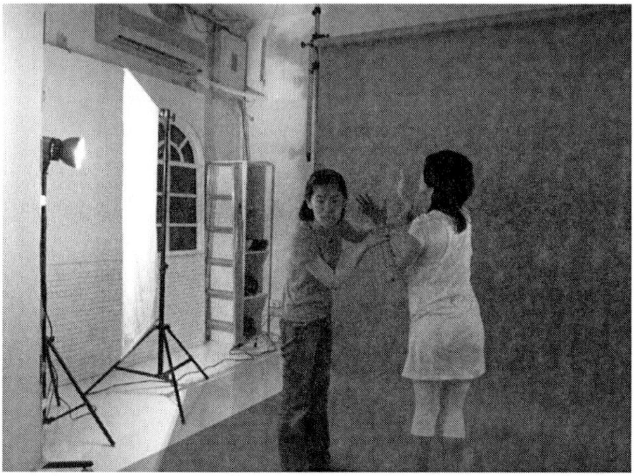

Fig. 3-4: While posing and shooting under the guidance of the stop motion software, the actor was as passive as a puppet. She needs someone to give her oral instruction or directly adjust her posture. She cannot look at the computer screen and gauged the position by herself.

As a result, the difficulty of bringing the pixilated figure and cartoon reference together made me pause and think: is there something incompatible between pixilation and cartoon's hyperrealism? Are pixilation and naturalistic animation so fundamentally different as to suggest they are related to different kinds of image systems altogether?

Therefore I embarked upon the following investigation: an attempt to explain the gap between pixilation and cartoon's hyperrealism. This also aimed at developing a strategy for pixilation to approach the cartoon style in my practice. Instead of looking at the difference between pixilation and cartoon style directly, I began the investigation with the comparison between pixilation and live action film, which seems to be a source of inspiration when cartoon wishes to aspire to a higher level of realism. In these comparisons, I recognised that pixilation and live action belong to different image systems.Whereas the smallest unit of the former is *the condensation of time*, that of the latter is *the dissection of time*. This not only added to my understanding of the essence of pixilated figure, but also helped me grasp some of pixilation's disassociation with the cartoon's realist principle. Nevertheless, the borders can be blurred or broken. By examining films with pixilation, two different ways of breaking the borders between the two systems are identified. Finally, the second integrating method, which is the revised version based on the new understandings from the comparisons, is introduced.

4.1 Comparing Stringed Photographs and Continuous Photogram

As introduced in chapter 1, although pixilation has similarities with live action, it is often categorised as a kind of animation. In pixilation, humans are photographed frame by frame and become like objects or puppet in a mechanical process. Therefore, one obvious difference between pixilation and live action is that the former is made by stop-frame photography and the later by a rolling camera without interruption. Since a pixilation sequence is like a pile of photographs put together, the comparison between pixilation and live action film would become a comparison between stringed photographs and continuous *photogramme(s)*, a term Gill Deleuze uses in his *Cinema 1: The Movement Image* (1986) to indicate an individual still frame taken from the motion-picture film.

Aiming at understanding the difference between pixilated and live-action images, this section compares the concepts of stringed photos and continuous photograms by focusing on three aspects: (1) closed and open forms, (2) detached and immanent elements, and (3) different attitudes towards the unseen.

Closed and Open Forms

In the 1920s, Oskar Fischinger in the early days of his career, conceived an interesting approach to make abstraction in motion: firstly to put colour liquids and three-dimensional modelling materials together to build up a block of colour wax, and then put the moulded wax block in a machine which cut thin slices off the surface of the block. After each slice was cut off, a camera placed before the machine photographed the surface of the cross-plane. The next slice was then cut off, and again the new cross-plane was photographed. The result is fascinating with those shades and shapes in ever-changing patterns. Yet a single photograph itself is not really pretty or striking. Fischinger's approach is a good example of the "open form" I refer to here. Though photographed separately, the image of each slice exhibits a great sense of flexibility and fluidity that fills the gap between the photographs with a strong implication of continuity.

The concept of open and closed forms is often used by art historians and critics. Film theorists use this concept to understand the composition of cinematic images. For example, Giannetti (2011: 83-84) suggests that in open-form images, the frame tends to be de-emphasised to signify that more important information lies outside the edges of the composition, whereas in closed forms, space seems enclosed and self-contained rather than continuous. However, here I wish to use the concept to indicate the continuity between frames rather than shots; this is because one of the subjects of this study is animation, and the smallest and most basic unit of it is a *frame*, not a *shot*.

The composition of each still from Fischinger's wax experiments exhibits a sense of incompleteness and a lack of emphasis. Its accidental, "found" look also typifies open forms. On the other hand, a metaphor of closed forms comes from *Fallen Art* (2004), an award-winning animated short made by Polish director Tomasz Bagiński. In *Fallen Art*, General A is making an animated film in a forgotten military base. His art consists of a twisted method of stop-motion photography, in which the individual frames of his film are created by photographs of the bodies of dead soldiers who are pushed down by a sergeant from a tower onto a slab of concrete. Through dubbing in tango music, the dead bodies in the stringed photographs seem to dance feverishly, though with jiggled movement. This is an exemplary expression of closed forms. Each frame includes only one unique dead body along with the blood splats. Every single frame thus forms a closed, isolated world in General A's moving piece. In this sense I feel quite sure that pixilated film belongs to closed forms. In contrast, the cartoon film, though made of series of individual drawings or paintings, often shows great continuity and may appear more like open forms.

Clancy (1991: 258) believes that the techniques of animation do not rely on a continuous substrate of real movement, and that the movements created by animation depend only on the radical discontinuity of the images. Animation movements, as Clancy comments, "are predicated on the multiplication and assemblage of transcendentally discontinuous figures in a heterogeneous space-time rather than upon the segmentation and reconstruction of continuous and homogeneous movement." Therefore he argues, "Animation is the multiplication of worlds at 24 worlds per second." Of course they are drawings made separately, yet where does the sense of continuity of the drawing sequence come from? I think cartoon films have clever ways to blur the distinctions between individual drawings. Although comprised of drawings that take painstaking efforts to create, cartoon film has developed strategies which could effectively break down the isolation of each drawing. Included in the golden principles, strategies such as "squash and stretch", "overlapping action" and the "follow-through" can increase the continuity between drawings; "breaking joints" is fundamental for creating flexibility; and "dry brush" is a way to emulate the transparency of live action blur movement. For traditional hand-drawn animation, where the cartoon's realistic principle matured, these strategies are easily applied since a drawn figure is easy to distort or manipulate. Cartoon films not only have a range of tools to extend the continuity between originally separated frames, they search for continuity to achieve greater realism. In contrast, flexible, changeable and flowing lines and shapes are more difficult to apply to pixilated images. The discontinuity between pixilated frames is, in contrast, persistent. This perhaps was one of the basic reasons that made the result of my first integration attempt jiggle considerably. While trying to pose, frame by frame, to simulate the drawing reference, what concerned me most during the acting was the similarity between my pose and the drawn figure on each single frame, rather than the continuity between the frames. In this way the poses in my first attempt became isolated, closed forms.

Detached and Immanent Elements

In the first of his two volumes on cinema, *The Movement-Image*, Deleuze (1986: 2) speaks of the relationship between movement and image in a photogram: "Cinema proceeds with photogrammes – that is, with immobile sections – twenty-four images per second. But it has often been noted that what it gives us is not the photogramme; it is an intermediate image, to which movement is not appended or added, the movement on the contrary belongs to the intermediate image as immediate given. In short, cinema does not give us an image to which movement is added, it immediately gives us a movement-image." Photographs and photograms are both captures of a very short time, or an instant. In Deleuze's account, they appear to belong to two distinctive approaches in terms of the relationships between instant and movement. Henry Bergson (1911: 305) was the first to distinguish different ways of reconstituting movement from instants: the ancient and the modern. On the one hand, for antiquity, "movement refers to intelligible elements, Forms or Ideas which are themselves eternal and immobile" (Deleuze 1986: 4). Movement conceived in this way is a series of poses or privileged instants, as in classical dance or photography. On the other hand, the modern way has been realised by scientific achievement which enables a camera to capture movement at regular and intensively rapid intervals. Modern movement is related not to privileged instants, but to "any-instant-whatever" in Deleuze's term. Unlike that in paintings or long-exposure photographs, the pose or instant in these photograms is at the same time an analysis and a synthesis of the movement, i.e. the instant results in and from motion. The pose in the snapshot of a passing reality is *immanent* to the continuity of the movement. This is why Deleuze (1986: 4) states that, for modern cinema, "although movement was still recomposed, *it was no longer recomposed from formal transcendental elements (poses), but from immanent material elements (sections)*."

In light of Deleuze's account, the earliest photogram would be the chronophotographic experiments of Étienne-Jules Marey and Eadweard James Muybridge in the nineteenth century (fig. 3-5). They are considered to be directly related to modern cinema (Clancy 1991; Broadfoot & Butler 1991). Even in the pre-cinematic period, the dissection of a horse's gallop made by Marey's graphic recordings and Muybridge's equidistant snapshots proved their dependency on movement. However, to consider these photograms as animation poses for the part I wish to note about pixilation is too simplistic and can be misleading; because the poses for pixilation are constructed as still images, not the result of a sequence.

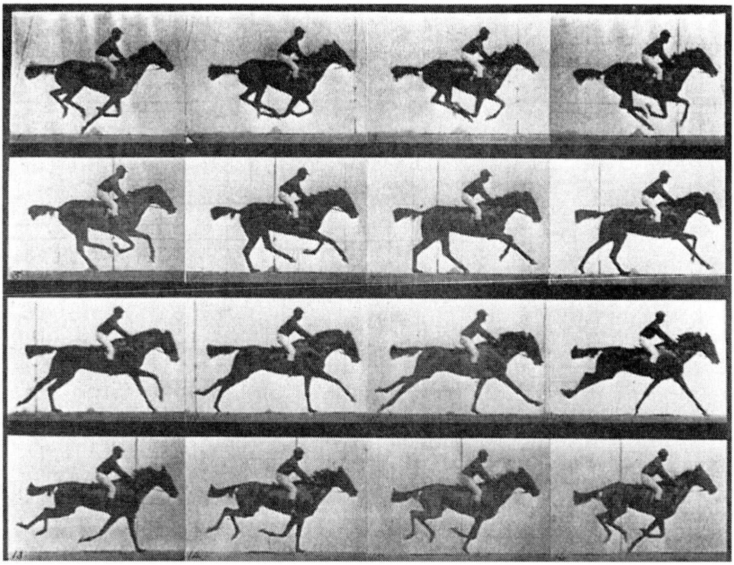

Fig. 3-5: Photographs of galloping horse, by Eadweard Muybridge, 1978

For pixilation, the technique of photographing a live-actor's poses one by one and then stringing them together to form the illusion of movement, poses and movement are detached. The movement indicated by the stringed photographs, or a series of photos that are strung together, is not what is embodied in the model's poses. This is especially significant when stop motion software is used to map and adjust the poses. The positions of the model's torso and limbs are all guided by the software, for the model cannot even read the information on the computer screen by her/himself and needs someone else to give spoken instructions or adjust her/his limbs directly. The model is thus as passive as a puppet, losing any sense of positioning. Moreover, as the process of position adjusting and capturing on a computer could take minutes for each photograph, the model has to remain immobile over an extended period of time so that the tiredness and impulse to give in to gravity, I feel, become almost visible. Pixilation as such presents an apparent detachment between pose and movement.

Stop-motion software was indispensible to my first approach at integrating pixilation and cartoon's hyperrealism. However, with this software the discordance of the vital forces in the moment increases, and the contradiction between pixilation and the system of "any-instant-whatever" is enhanced too. Here a question arises: Since cartoon animation, in contrast with most pixilation animation, can achieve a rather high degree of naturalism, does it belong to the system of any-instant-whatever rather than that of privileged instant? Deleuze may be read as suggesting an affirmative answer. Although Deleuze says very little about animation, there is a a paragraph considering the relation of the cartoon film to cinema. For Deleuze (1986: 5), the reason the cartoon film is not foreign to cinema is that it does not proceed from the synthesis of poses photographed one by one. Of cartoon film he says,

> …the drawing no longer constitutes a pose or a completed figure, but the description of a figure which is always in the process of being formed or dissolving through the movement of lines and points taken at any-instant-whatevers of their course. The cartoon film is related not to a Euclidean, but to a Cartesian geometry. It does not give us a figure described in a unique moment, but the continuity of the movement which describes the figure. (ibid.)

The above statement reveals a controversial view. First, there are numerous kinds of animation, and what is in Deleuze's mind might only be the more live-action oriented/imitative cartoon films. Second, the construction of movement in animation, even in the most successful demonstration of cartoon's realistic principle, is an intelligible synthesis rather than the sensible analysis that occurs in "any-instant-whatevers". With strategies such as the golden principles, animation poses could give an impression that they arethe results of motion, that they are inseparable from the continuity of the movement. Yet the poses are not intrinsically *immanent* to the movement, as animators have the freedom to choose whether they want to emulate "any instant-whatever" or not. For pixilation animation, it is more difficult to apply those cartoon principles to pixilated figures. But pixilation may have its own advantage in giving the impression of "any instant-whatever". After all, the frames are not necessarily constructed by photos that are taken from poses detached with movement. They can still be poses taken from corresponding movement and then be edited on a frame-by-frame basis; in this way, the continuity of the movement would be retained and play a role in "describing the figure" as Deleuze states in the previous quote. That is, the filmmaker can choose whether the poses are dependant on corresponding movement or detached from it, although the latter may be pixilation in a more strict sense.

Mike Jittlov's 1979 short *The Wizard of Speed and Time* shows both kinds of construction. Like most of Jittlov's films, he performs in this film himself. Wearing a green wizard costume, he runs across various landscaps at super speed to present "the wizard of speed", and then brings life in magical ways to inanimate objects on a film stage to show "the wizard of time". The performance of these two sections, the wizard of speed and the wizard of time, are constructed using different techniques. The first seems mainly constructed through poses shot in corresponding movement. Through changing frame rates or extracting and editing the frames, the illusion of hyper-speed is created. The second is mainly constructed through sequences of still poses that are detached from the corresponding movement and separate from each other. In this way each instant is a priviledged moment that, when put together, the sequence of priviledged moments appears to be scenes full of magic.

In my first attempt, the poses were made and shot separately rather than in their corresponding movement. They were pixilation with privileged instants. I realised that the "live-action animation" I was looking for does not necessarily include only the privileged instants. Therefore for the second attempt, I used pixilation in a broader sense that incorporates poses dependent on movement. The methods are introduced in the last part of this chapter.

Different Attitudes toward the Unseen

In live-action footage, no matter how fast the shutter speed is, or how strong the implication of continuity the footage provides, something is always missing, invisible in the interval between any two frames. ZbigniewRybczynski, the creator of *Tango* (1983), states: "I don't like to draw distinctions between film recorded at different speeds. Even twenty-four frames per second is a form of stop-motion – there are breaks in the movements between frames" (quoted in Solomon 1987: 11). The space between frames, the unseen rather than the visualised, is foregrounded.

Although differing significantly in their methods and concerns, the chronophotographic experiments of Marey and Muybridge and the pixilation in Švankmajer's*Picnic with Weissmann*(1968)can be discussed in relation to "the unseen", where two different kinds of attitudes can be recognised.

Marey and Muybridge can be seen as pioneers of cinema. During the late 1870s Muybridge successfully captured instantaneous motion in a series of plates. A review of Muybridge's first exhibition states how the camera enabled us to comprehend what was concealed (Mike & Daniel 1989: 142). Marey's concern was also to create machines to make visible what until then had remained invisible. The interest in invisibility led Marey toward an investment in the machinic (Manning 2009: 83). Marey's relation to the nineteenth-century debate on the "decadent body" in France is worth mentioning here. After France's defeat in the Franco-Prussian War (1870-1871), heightened anxiety focused on the degenerate or decadent body raised, and the gymnastic movement emerged in France. Marey's chronophotography can be seen as a direct response to the decadent body, as a means to reveal and acquire imperceptible physiological information, so as to devise a system of physical training for a new healthy and efficient body (Braun 1994: 70-71). Marey wanted to study bodies in their movement, in their "livingness" (fig.3-6). In Marey's time, many scholars, such as French physiologist Claude Bernard (1813-76), believed that the best way to gain biological knowledge was to dissect and study corpses instead of living bodies. Behind this attitude was the idea that deep contemplation of truth meant withdrawing the body from the world, from the movement of life, so as to freeze its vital functions and allow the mind to leave the body in search of knowledge. Rejecting this idea, Marey insisted on investigating an organism in its kinetics (Dagognet 1992: 58). In a positivist manner, Marey believed in the mechanics of what could be proven. His chronophotography worked not only to portray but also to master biology's movement, rendering visible its unseen motions and making evident its unconscious behaviour. The contemporaneous philosopher Henry Bergson challenged the positivism apparent in the philosophical framework of Victorian science which viewed the world as a sum of discrete objects that are observable and measurable. For Bergson, true knowledge cannot be reached through an analysis that fragments them. What is real is a unity that can only be known through "intuition" (Braun 1994: 279). In other words, what concerns Bergson most is the invisible and indivisible, which for him could never be found through an analytic approach.

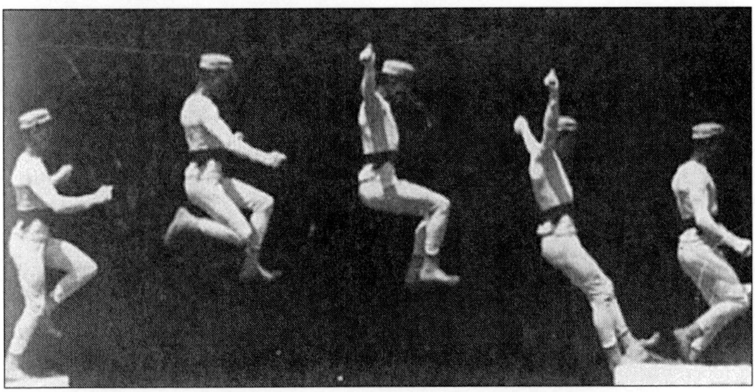

Fig. 3-6: Chronophotagraphy of high jump, by Etienne-Jules Marey, 1886

Living in the era of scientific theories of relativity, radio waves, x-rays, radiation, widespread electricity and other invisible forces, both Marey and Bergson had an interest in the unseen, and found the eye insufficient for obtaining knowledge. For Marey the world lays beyond the reach of the eye. A machine was needed to overcome its frailty. For Bergson, the eye is too similar to a camera as it automatically stops and fixes objects that flow into its realm of action, and thus can only provide an incomplete view of reality (Braun 1994: 280). Reality, in Bergson's view, could never be known by being made visible. This attitude inspired generations of artists. When high-speed cameras with the amazing ability to film up to a quarter of a million frames per second are developed to dig deeper into the unseen space between any-instant-whatevers, pixilated films preserve that space to reflect or exploit another kind of invisibility. Sometimes the absent is the most "present", as can be seen in the situation of Mr.Weissmann in Svankmajer's stop-motion short *Picnic with Weissmann* (1968). This unusual picnic presents delightful scenes of a phonograph playing records, chairs playing cards, desks passing a balloon, and clothes sunbathing. No human is shown, but signs of their existence from photographs on the wardrobe can be recognised. As the picnic proceeds, the doubt increases: where is the human? Finally the puzzle is solved when a man bound and gagged in underwear appears, falling out of the wardrobe into the grave arranged by those autonomous objects. Although he has been kept hidden and only appears in the last scene, the man is actually the centre of our concerns throughout the film. It is not rare in pixilated films that things are made even more visible through their invisibility. For example, in Chuck Menville's and Len Janson's *Vicious Cycles* (1967), a gang of tough-looking cyclists roam the highways on invisible bikes leaving visible tire tracks, and then lose the girl to the riders of children's scooters which are invisible as well. The motorcycles and the scooters – the technologies that are unseen – are the real protagonists. Born at a point of the history in which the convergence of technology, industry and capitalism created an unprecedentedly confusing and complex world, cinema not only captures the shocks and sensations of a new world, but also portrays the agonistic aspect of a spiritual struggle. Pixilated figures, by retrieving the space as well as the tension between inner and external forces, could be seen as an expressive agency of human's spiritual status/states in the modern world.

4.2 Breaking the Borders between the Two Systems

In the previous discussions I looked at the possible distinctions between pixilation and live action from different perspectives. There seem to be two different image systems: one belongs to the dissection of time and the other the condensation of time. However, cartoon is an art form hovering between these two systems. Bill Schaffer (2005: 84-85) points out that animation introduces a double register of time: the manual temporality of composition of individual drawings, and the automatic temporality of the completed animated sequence. Filmmakers such as Mike Jittlov use both poses detached from movement and those dependent on it in his films. Choosing between the dissection and condensation of time is not an either-or option in filmmaking. Even without the digital, filmmakers can still find ways to blur the distinctions. Many of the works of Jeff Scher, a painter and experimental filmmaker, are examples of breaking down the borders between the dissection and condensation of time without digital technologies. His recent work *Pretty, Dead* (2010) that is appropriated from a range of live action cinematic sources is a homage to the narratives of film noir. Favouring vintage machinery and technologies, Scher is famous for using the traditional rotoscopic technique. Described by himself as "motion paintings", his use of rotoscoping differs from that seen in both mainstream cartoons (e.g. the Fleischer Brothers' Koko series) and experimental ones (e.g. works by Gerrit van Dijk). In most rotoscope-based animation, the drawn image takes liberties with the physical appearance of bodies depicted in the original, cinematographic source. However, in Scher's films, the bodies are rendered faithful to their iconic original in the live-action source. Sometimes a viewer can even recognise the live-action source of the motions. Despite this fidelity, Scher treats each successive frame of film as a separate, individual painting. He amplifies the effect of perceptual discontinuity within the actions portrayed by creating successive images that contain significantly different graphic details (Fore 2007). In other words, for Scher, the live-action sections do not serve as a form of assistance in creating smooth and continuous movement for exaggerated, animated virtual figures, but rather a continuum that needs to be broken up and violated. Viewers witness in Scher's works a visual paradox: a series of brief but entirely uninterrupted motions that are simultaneously aggressively fragmented.

One of the impacts that digital technologies on the moving image may have had is they have provided new ways to collapse borders between the condensation of time and the dissection of time. Cyriak's *Cows & Cows & Cows* (2010) is a demonstration of how the gaps between still images are erased through the use of computer software. In this surreal, bizarre work, cattle grazing peacefully on the meadow start to move with the beat. At first the cows only nod heads, bend knees or step up and down, then they begin the crazy transformation of stretching, shrinking, melting, and restructuring: at one moment becoming huge spider cows and at another becoming a growing molecular geometry. At the end, as the electronic music calms down, they turn back into cattle grazing peacefully on the meadow. Transformation in this work happens smoothly and "naturalistically" between poses, no matter how irrelevant they are to each other. Cyriak is a renowned creator of internet content. Using only the most commonly available software such as Adobe Photoshop and After Effect for digital compositing, Cyriak breaks the discontinuity between poses in a strong and violent way.

It is also worth noting that although the kaleidoscopic effects as seen in Scher's works can be created by digital tools, the use of digital tools would generate different meaning. The New York-based artist Madame Chao's video art is an example. The artist's incoherent imagery is created by computer software and programming. He achieves this by sampling seemingly random fragments of video games, noise blasts and pulsating techno beats, and mixing them with scenes from cult-classic Asian flicks and odd outtakes from contemporary America, including scenes from TV commercials. Similar to what we can see in Scher's films, the incoherent images form an intense, chaotic melee that suggests the whirling frames of a kaleidoscope, yet somehow manages to remain both cohesive and compelling. Both Scher's and Madame Chao's works break the linearity and continuity of the found footage. The major difference between them is that the "discontinuity" of Madame Chao's work derives from the use of computer algorithms. The concepts of the media's materiality are different. What Madame Chao's work represents is not the random scattering of images between two points in the timeline, but a multiplied warping of the path between the two points.

The above cases show various ways that independent filmmakers have used to change the relations between poses and movement, so as to break the borders between dissection and condensation of time. As mentioned earlier, cartoon's hyperrealism can create the impression of any-instant-whatever, in which the dissection and condensation of time are blurred for each single frame/drawing. To emulate cartoon's hyperrealism, the pixilated figure shall also present the ability to break the borders. Digital tools can be useful in serving this purpose.

4.3 Integrating Pixilation with Cartoon's Hyprerealism

The above investigation reveals some of the characteristics of pixilation based on the relations between poses and movement. Now I can proceed to the main question: how do I integrate pixilation with cartoon's hyperrealistic style? Pixilation tends to be the condensation of time or poses detached with their corresponding movement, perhaps a fundamental cause of the gap between pixilation and cartoon's hyperrealism in my first attempt to bring them together. Therefore, the question may be asked in another way: how do I break down the isolation of each photo in a pixilation film? Pixilation does not have the same capacity of drawn animation to distort or incomplete the shape or line of the figures. It needs its own way to achieve hyperrealism.

A set of approaches are developed in my second method in combining pixilation and cartoon's hyperrealism, where three points are stressed. Firstly, the actor should decide the posing and moving by her/himself, rather than stand there and wait to be arranged or adjusted. If the actor is passive like a puppet and does not know about the next move, the muscles and other details of her/his body will clearly reveal this lack of sense of direction and as a result will separate poses and movement. Secondly, for the same reason the actors will not pause for each shot, instead they will be shot in their movement. Lastly, digital compositing will be used to enhance the continuity and the sense of force of the movement.

Below are the steps of the second method, which relies strongly on digital tools. Apart from the digital compositing part, the re-arrangement of the timing and spacing on a frame-by-frame basis could hardly be achieved without the computer.

- Firstly ask the actors to perform actions like waving hands, turning around, sneaky walking and lifting heavy stuff in their own way. Explain the cartoon principles to them, and ask them to perform the same actions using these principles. Compare and discuss the differences of their performances with them.
- Next ask the actors to study the selected cartoon clips carefully. Examine the key poses and the performing style together.
- Next, shoot in front of a green screen: the actors represent the movement of the cartoon clips in continual but very slow motion, neglecting issues of timing, concentrating only in the expression of key poses and exaggerations.
- Make exposure sheets to re-define the timing and spacing of each action.
- Render and export the raw footage into photograph sequences, pick out the photographs (poses) and re-arrange them into a new sequence according to the exposure sheet, thus to form movements that can express the sense of momentum (fig. 3-7).
- Enhance the sense of momentum by using some of the cartoon's strategy. Breaking joints, in this project, proved to be a useful tool to increase the flexibility and openness of pixilation figures. A bit of digital transformation could benefit the continuity of movement.
- Replace part of the figures with drawn elements to produce an extremely exaggerated effect such as a squashed face.

The result is presented in the last scenes of *Flying Tunes*, from time code

7'00" to 8'00", where the two protagonists are annoyed by the fly and begin the action to beat it. Their cartoony movements are the integration of live-action shooting and frame-by-frame manipulation, which is an attempt to break the borders between the dissection and the condensation of time, and hopefully would produce the effect of estrangement in both live action and cartoon.

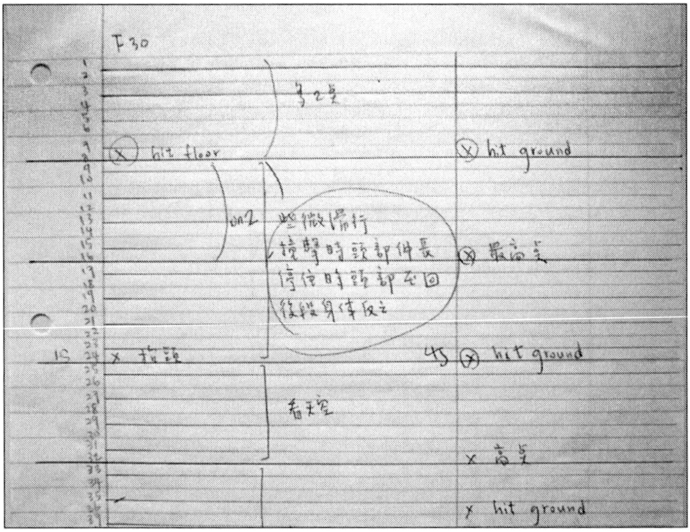

Fig. 3-7: Sample exposure sheet

In summary, cinema emerges from a dialectic between stillness and motion widely reflected in the visual culture of the turn of the century. Ancient philosophy gives time the quality of an illusionary double of the transcendental elements. Modern science breaks time down as "any-instances-whatever". For Deleuze, cinema occupies a transitional phase between these two moments in philosophy. Originating from a curiosity that emerged in the process of the making of practice, the discussion begins with a question as to whether there is something that keeps the technique of pixilation alienated from cartoon's realist principles. Starting from a comparison of films composed of open frames with those composed of closed frames, this chapter examines the differences between realistic cartoon films and pixilated films. The point here is to focus on the specific properties of pixilation, the technique which is generally seen as a kind of animation but differs from the generally conceived idea of cartoon animation. In this chapter, the digital is considered in terms of the new ways it provides to break the borders between image systems based on the dissection and condensation of time. Instead of suggesting that there are indestructible boundaries between the two modes of image systems, or restrictions in applying the technique of pixilation, this investigation is intended to deepen the understanding of the tools animators are working with, and thus to develop a creative strategy in a more meaningful way. After all, the materiality of the media is not a fixed, unchanging stage on which the content of the film is played out. For example, the interrelationships between photographs and photograms could actually be part of the performance.

CONCLUSION

This research is an inquiry into the relationship between live action and animation in hybrid films, and the function of digital tools in this relationship. This involves asking how the integration of their opposing attributes might disrupt perceptual realism and produce a sense of estrangement in a meaningful way. Issues raised throughout this process of enquiry are elaborated in the themes of the four chapters. The first is a general consideration of the nature of the relationship between live action and animation. The second and third suggest two tropes in investigating hybrid efforts that are tested mainly through the use of the pixilated figure. In devising various kinds of pixilation a number of practical/technical problems were encountered, so the fourth theme was thus elaborated to explain and solve one of the significant problems. The four themes are explored in considerable depth while maintaining a unified and coherent structure with an increasingly detailed focus (fig. 5-1).

The intention of this research has been to re-evaluate the interface between live action and animation, in order to break away from the dominant aesthetics of digital cinema and re-consider it as a formal force within moving images in relation to the effects introduced by digital technologies. The four chapters of this thesis and my own creative work on the characteristics of the animation-live action interface have revealed and emphasised that, rather than being a determined entity, the interface functions as a condition through which particular experiences are generated. These experiences are based on the double and fluctuating nature of the co-presence of live action and animation. The relationship between them is always a dynamic oscillation of negation and supplementation. The permeable interplay between emergent and receding aspects inherent in the interface makes it a site of transformation where the dialogue between live action and animation is both the source of visual codes used in the construction of meaning and the formal force through which the spatial and temporal elements are structured for the production of each frame.

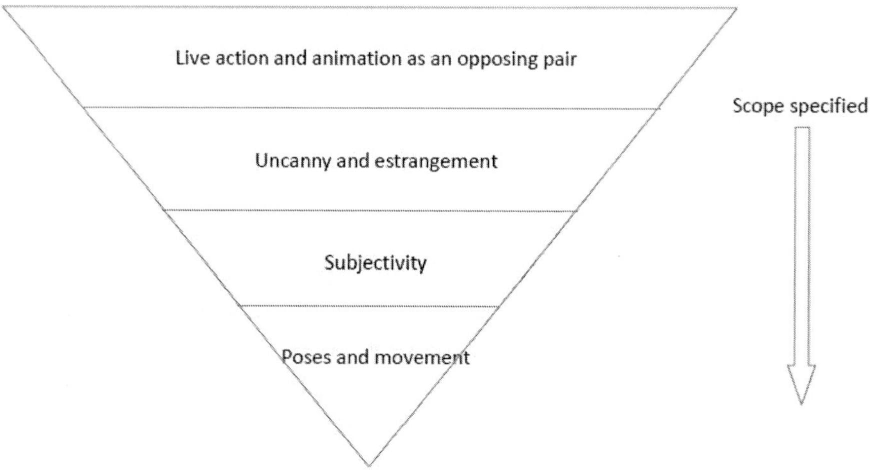

Fig. 5-1: The four themes in this research are explored in a coherent structure with an increasingly detailed focus.

In contextualising the nature of the interface and discovering its functions and meanings, within the digital in particular, I focussed on two underlying themes: (1) the uncanniness of the co-presence, and (2) the expression of subjectivity through this co-presence.

The first theme concerns the integration of live action and animation as an operation of the experience of the supplementary, and connects the interface with the uncanny. This concept of the interface is intrinsically linked to cinema's relation to the Enlightenment and modernity, where cinema manifests itself as a historical entity. With the varying and transforming experience of new digital technologies under changing social conditions, the interface has the capacity to address a collective/individual imaginary and thus can play a potentially subversive role. Thinking about the above concepts from the standpoint of a Far-Eastern Asian filmmaker, there is a mutation between the effects of hyperrealisation and derealisation – feeling unreal toward the real and real toward the unreal – that makes fluid the apparently contrasting connections between the authentic and imaginative, with their binary oppositions multiplied and obscured.

The second theme shows that one of the major characteristics and strengths of this hybrid practice lies in the reflection and expression of subjectivity. The struggle of subjectivity can be exposed by the objective progressive drive inherent in hybrid works. In this respect, more weight could be added to the interface's relation to the idea of an unstable duality, especially in the discussion of techniques and functions of hybridised characters. Through the operation of a hybridised subjectivity, the second theme is linked to the filmmaker's existential condition, characterised by a continuously adjusted subjectivity.

In realising this hybridised subjectivity the technique of pixilation was conceived in order to be integrated with a cartoon style. It was achieved by reconstructing pixilation from the concept of stringing photographs to that of a series of photograms. The resulting hybridised figure is neither pixilation nor cartoon. It is something that simultaneously obscures and brings to light the different codes of live action and animation, i.e. an entity that makes much of the interface's quality of a doubled duality – seen as an integration of two "becomings" as illustrated/discussed in the Introduction.

Theorising that the interface highlights at least two aspects of early films, namely notions of uncanniness and subjectivity, embodies the stories of modernity and the birth of cinema. As stated in Chapter 2, the uncanny is a distinctively modern experience although its roots can be tracked back to the Enlightenment. According to Collins and Jervis (2008: 5), the uncanny has become "a key term for figuring the uncertainties, tensions and obscurities of modernity itself". The idea of subjectivity is also strongly related to the concept of modernity. As argued by Ferguson (2000:3), the definition of modernity is characterised by traits such as autonomy, creativity, and freedom; and the genesis of modernity can be traced to the emergence of subjectivity. As with technology, industrialisation, obligatory schooling, clinical hygiene, among others, the ideas of the uncanny and subjectivity are actually rather recent inventions that emerged only in the nineteenth and twentieth centuries. The uncanny and subjectivity are two different aspects of modernity.

As a perceived shift has occurred in the general experience of culture and transformed modernity into a phase comprehended as late modernism or postmodernism, the exploration of the uncanny and subjectivity should also have signalled this shift. This research responds to this shift by examining the effect of estrangement as the derealisation of virtual reality. Suspended in indeterminacy and ambiguity, the uncanniness of the hybridised figure can be sources of derealisation that links aesthetic and existential estrangement and leads us to a derealisation of hyperreality in the real world. Regarding the concept of subjectivity, in modern times the idea of individuality and subjectivity has become rather prominent. I am the subject of my own experiences, feelings and opinions. The individual is the centre of her or his own world, and not just the periphery of a socially constructed world. However, this centred self and the extreme freedom it promised have promoted the fragmented or decentred self of postmodernity. This is not only observed by many scholars (Ferguson 2000; Jameson 1991), but also a real life experience of my own and of many other people of my generation. In our era the very notion of a stable self or subject has been called into question. The stable centre of the self seems to be replaced by multiple centres with different perspectives. This is reflected in the discussions in this thesis, and is expressed through my practice.

The interface has an enduring role in the aesthetics and development of moving images. The doubled duality inherent in the interface underlines an obscuring and overlapping of the contradictory constructedness it brings into being. Working with moving images using digital tools means that the interface is even more unstable and mutable.The images can continue to be developed, edited and reconstructed, not only in terms of the tensions between live-action/animated elements but also in relation to performance codes. I feel the use of the interface does not only confuse and disturb visual integration such as perceptual realism, but it is also a way in which I can articulate my thinking about issues such as cultural identity, which can be seen as political. The displacement of the interface keeps the roles of live action and animation dynamic, denying either of them a position of absolute marginality or centrality.

Contributions

This thesis makes a contribution to the field of independent filmmaking in terms of reconsidering the interface between live action and animation in its relationship to cinema and technology. The contribution is enriched by the discussion of the aesthetic and cultural implications that develop between practices encountered in this research (not just my own but including those referenced in this thesis). Through the submission of practical work and textual analysis I demonstrated the potential of theoretical and philosophical contexts to establish a methodology for independent filmmaking, where a cyclic process is the fundamental framework. Finding potential meanings for the employment of the interface has led to a network of ideas, starting with the uncanniness of hybrid films and modernity, to the effects of estrangement and derealisation, the construction of subjectivity, and related implications in the formation of hybridised figures. The exploration of the aesthetics of estrangement and the expression of subjectivity in hybrid films led to an inquiry into cinematic time and movement, revealing another dimension to the difference and interrelationship between live action and animation. In both the practical work and the text, I approach the effect of derealisation through the operation of the interface, where the intervention of digital technologies is considered.

A number of original findings were shown in the discussions of the four themes in the thesis's four chapters. In Chapter 1 in the definitions of live action and animation, I identified their interdependence and opposing qualities. The performance of contemporary computer-generated imagery was analysed in terms of its links with traditional special effects under the categories of effect, non-human character, pseudo-human character and human character animation. A double-faced disposition in digital imaging technology was then suggested and argued. Chapter 2 confirmed the importance of the concept of the uncanny in understanding the interface between live action and animation, and added a dimension relating to the manipulation of the interface through the establishment and operation of an experience of the supplementary. It was suggested that this dimension is promising in terms of derealising the virtual and the real existential world. Chapter 3 recognised and showed that subjectivity is a substantial topic in historical live-action and animation hybrid films. Along with the exemplification of my own practice, subjectivity is argued to be an effective trope in hybrid film practice. Although self-figuration has been recognised as a significant characteristic of hybrid films, especially early works, this research argued that there may be a gender difference in depicting the relationship between animator and animated: the struggle between the creator and the creature appears less often and has a less conflictual nature in works by female filmmakers. In addition, the way this research connects tensions between internal/external with the establishment of subjectivity in hybrid films has rarely been discussed in an academic context. Chapter 4 demonstrated that the experiment of integrating pixilation and cartoon style could lead animators to a deeper understanding of cinematic time and movement. It showed that the difference between live action and animation does not necessarily lie in the photographic or graphic. When considering the relation between poses and movement, sometimes the graphic, which in this case refers to mainstream cartoon films, might be more closely related to live action than the photographic, which is pixilation in this study. It also showed how theoretical enquiry can emerge directly from the making of practice in an art research.

Another original contribution may lie in my approach to integrating the making of practice and the establishment of theory. By locating it in the cyclic process, the relationship between practice and theory extends the visual research and dilutes the contrast between them. Besides the theoretical findings pinpointed through the analysis of works by other artists and concepts, my own practice contributes to knowledge by inspiring, assessing and demonstrating ideas.

The researcher's experience of filmmaking within Taiwanese culture and then living and studying within a Western liberal humanities context may have endowed this research with a cross-cultural character. I hope this thesis is a demonstration that the anxiety induced by uncertainty can contribute to creative and intellectual activities – something that may have value and relevance to other overseas researchers/practitioners who come into a Western creative and pedagogical structure at the highest level of research (the Ph.D.).

Critical Review and Future Research

An asset of this research is the making of practice, and the breadth of literature and historical hybrid films which contribute to its findings. This study is very much inspired by the researcher's practice; therefore it provides a description of the expanded context of the practice which could be seen as a qualitative case study. This practice-led approach may be criticised for not having one unified, systematic analytical methodology and hence lacking potential for generalisation, but this study benefits from the application of a cyclic strategy which provides a more structured process for the generation and development of ideas.

Although a potential criticism of this method might be that the inclusion of the researcher's personal experience makes the discussion autobiographical, as a creative experience it is difficult and hardly feasible to divorce the practice from the maker's personal identity and feeling. In this thesis only the personal experiences that are significantly related to the creation of the practice are delineated.

Although the research described in this thesis inevitably has limitations it provides a substantial starting point from which to carry out future work from a cross-cultural perspective. There are many implications arising from this research for an Asian independent filmmaker. However, one unexplored issue that emerged from this study is a real bridge/dialogue between Western and Eastern standpoints. This poses an interesting subject for a future study: is it possible to explore estrangement, subjectivity, and the illusion of movement from the perspectives of Chinese philosophy? I hope this research does indeed suggest a starting place from which to begin to address this question.

BIBLIOGRAPHY

Books and articles

Adorno, T. W., 1984. *Aesthetic Theory*, translated by C. Lenhardt. London, Boston, Melbourne: Routledge & Kegan Paul.

Archer, B. 1995.The Nature of Research. *Co-Design*, 2: 6-13.

Armes, R., 1987. *Third World Film Making and the West*. Berkeley, Los Angeles, London: University of California Press.

Farquharson, A. S. L. trans., 1989.*The Meditations of Marcus Aurelieus Antoninus*. Oxford, New York: Oxford University Press.

Barnett, R., 2005. Recapturing the universal in the university. *Educational Philosophy and Theory*, Vol. 27, No. 6, pp. 785-797.

—. 2007. *A Will to Learn: being a student in an age of uncertainty*. Buckingham: Society for Research in Higher Education and Open University Press.

Baudrillard, J., 1983. *Simulacra and Simulation*, translated by S. F. Glaser. Michigan: The University of Michigan Press.

Bayne, S., 2008. Uncanny spaces for higher education: teaching and learning in virtual worlds. *ALT-J, Research in Learning Technology*, Vol. 16, No. 3, pp. 197-205.

Bazin, A., 2005. *What is Cinema?* Berkeley: University of California Press.

Bergson, H., 1911. *Creative Evolution*, translated by A. Mitchell. New York: Henry Holt.

Beckerman, H., 2003. *Animation: The Whole Story*. New York: Allworth Press.

Bolter, J.D. & R. Grusin, 1999.*Remediation: Understanding New Media*. Cambridge, MA: MIT Press.

Bordwell, D., 1985. *Narration in the Fiction Film*. Wisconsin: The University of Wisconsin Press.

Bordwell, D. & J. Staiger, 1985. Technology, style and mode of production. In: Bordwell, D., Staiger, J. & K. Thompson eds., *The Classical Hollywood Cinema.* London: Routledge.

Bordwell, D. & K. Thompson, 2008. *Film art: an Introduction,* 8th edition. Boston: McGraw Hill.

Bordwell, D. & K. Thompson, 2010. *Film art: an Introduction,* 10th edition. Boston: McGraw Hill.

Bouldin, J., 2001. The body, animation and the real: race, reality and the rotoscope in Betty Boop. In Koivunen, A. & Paasonen S. eds., Conference proceedings for *Affective Encounters: Rethinking Embodiment in Feminist Media Studies*. Available at: http://www.hum.utu.fi/oppiaineet/mediatutkimus/tutkimus/proceedings_pienennetty.pdf [Accessed22 Dec 2012]

Braun, M., 1994.*Picturing Time: Work of Etienne-Jules Marey (1830-1904)*. Chicago: University of Chicago Press.

Broadfoot, K. & R. Bulter, 1991. The illusion of illusion. In: A. Cholodenko ed., *The Illusion of Life: Essays on Animation*. Sydney: Power Publications, pp. 271-2.

Brooks, X., 2011. The Adventures of Tintin: The Secret of the Unicorn: review. *The Guardian*, [Online] 16 Oct 2011. Available at: http://www.guardian.co.uk/culture/2011/oct/16/tintin-adventures-secret-of-unicorn [Accessed 08 Sep 2012]

Buchanan, K., 2011. The biggest problem with the Tintin movie might be Tintin himself. *Vulture, NYMAG.COM*, [Online] 22 Jul 2011. Available at: http://www.vulture.com/2011/07/the_biggest_problem_with_the_t.html [Accessed 08 Sep 2012]

Burbank, J., & P. Steiner eds. and trans., 1977.*The Word and Verbal Art: Selected Essays by Jan Mukarovsky*. New Haven, CT: Yale University Press.

Burg, K., 2007.*Disney Refection Letter, 1938*.Image on Flicker [Online]. Available at: http://www.flickr.com/photos/polaroid/632255233/ [Accessed 22 Dec 2012]

Butte, G., 2004. *I Know That You Know That I Know: Narrating Subjects from "Moll Flanders" to "Marnie"*. Columbus: Ohio State University Press.

—.2008. Suture and the Narration of Subjectivity in Film. *Poetics Today*, 29(2): 277-308.

Cangialosi, J., 2011. *Rise of the Planet of the Apes* in the Uncanny Valley. Yahoo! Movies, [Online] 18 Aug 2011. Available at: http://movies.yahoo.com/news/rise-planet-apes-uncanny-valley-011200003.html [Accessed 20 Sep 2012].

Castle, T., 1997.Interview with Terry Castle, conducted by Michael Arnzen. In *The Return of the Uncanny*, special issue of *Paradoxa: Studies in World Literary Genres*, vol. 3, no. 3-4: 521-6.

Culhane, S., 1986.*Talking Animals and Other People*. New York: St. Martin's Press.

—.1988. *Animation: from Script to Screen*. New York: St. Martin's Press.

Cholodenko, A., 1991a. Introduction. In: A. Cholodenko ed., *The Illusion*

of Life: Essays on Animation. Sydney: Power Publications.
—.1991b. Who framed Roger rabbit, or the framing of animation. In: *The Illusion of Life: Essays on Animation*. Sydney: Power Publication.
Cholodenko, A. ed., 2007.*The Illusion of Life 2: More Essays on Animation*. Sydney: Power Publications.
Clancy, K., 1991. ΠΡΗΣΤΗΡ: The T(r)opology of Pyromania. In: A. Cholodenko ed., *The Illusion of Life: Essays on Animation.* Sydney: Power Publications in association with the Australian Film Commission.
Castle, T., 1995.*The Female Thermometer: Eighteenth-century Culture and the Invention of the Uncanny*. Oxford: Oxford University Press.
Chang, V., 1998.Wang's world. *Taiwan Review* [Website]. Available at: http://taiwanreview.nat.gov.tw/ct.asp?xItem=1281&CtNode=1369 [Accessed 11 Oct 2012].
Clinton, P., June 20, 2003. Hulk not quite all there. *CNN Entertainment*, [Online] 20 Jun 2003. Available at: http://articles.cnn.com/2003-06-19/entertainment/sprj.cas03.review.hulk_1_military-base-hulk-bruce-banner?_s=PM:SHOWBIZ [Accessed 07 Sep 2012].
Collins, J. & J. Jervis, 2008. Introduction. In: J. Collins & J. Jervis eds., *Uncanny Modernity: Cultural Theories, Modern Anxieties*. New York: Palgrave Macmillan.
Crafton, D., 1982. *Before Mickey*. Chicago: University of Chicago Press.
Crary, J., 1992. *Techniques of the Observer: On Vision and Modernity in the 19th Century*. Cambridge, Massachusetts: MIT Press.
Dagognet, F., 1992.*Etienne-Jules Marey: a passion for the trace*. New York: Zone Books.
Dargis, M., 2005.A savage and sexy city of pulp fiction regulars.*The New York Times*, [Online] 1 Apr 2005. Available at: http://movies.nytimes.com/2005/04/01/movies/01sin.html?adxnnl=1&adxnnlx=1278867634-d1VOFURCUvWbvELe7Ma4ew [Accessed 11 Oct 2012].
—. 2007. Confronting the fabled monster, not to mention his naked mon. *The New York Times*, [Online] 16 Nov, 2007. Available at: http://movies.nytimes.com/2007/11/16/movies/16beow.html?_r=0 [Accessed 05 Oct 2012].
—. 2010. Splice (2010). *The New York Times*, [Online] 03 Jun 2010. Available at: http://movies.nytimes.com/2010/06/04/movies/04splice.html?ref=movies [Accessed 18 Sep 2012].
—. 2011.The Adventures of Tintin (2011).*The New York Times*, [Online] 20 Dec 2011. Available at: http://movies.nytimes.com/2011/12/21/movies/the-adventures-of-tintin

-by-steven-spielberg-review.html?partner=rss&emc=rss&_r=0moc.semityn.seivom [Accessed 08 Sep 2012].

Darley, A., 2000. *Visual Digital Culture: Surface Play and Spectacle in New Media Genres*. London and New York: Routledge.

Dayan, D., 1974. The tutor-code of classical cinema. *Film Quarterly* 28: 22-31.

Deleuze, G., 1986. *Cinema 1: The Movement Image*, translated by H. Tomlinson & B. Habberjam. Minneapolis: University of Minnesota Press.

—.2004. *Desert Islands and Other Texts, 1953-1974*, edited by D. Lapoujade, translated by M. Taormina. New York: Semiotext(e).

Deleuze, G. & F. Guattari, 1987. *A Thousand Plateaus: Capitalism and Schizophrenia*. Minnesota: The University of Minnesota Press.

Derrida, J., 1981. Interview with Jean-Louis Houdebine and Guy Scarpetta. In: *Positions*, translated by A. Bass. Chicago: The University of Chicago Press, pp. 42-44.

Dick, B. 1999.*Qualitative Action Research: Improving the Rigour and Economy* [Website]. Available at: www.scu.edu.au/schools/gcm/ar/arp/rigour2.html. [Accessed June 2009].

Dolar, Mladen. 1991. "I shall be with you on your wedding-night": Lacan and the uncanny. *October*, vol. 58: 5-23.

Kristeva, J., 1991. *Strangers to Ourselves*. London: Harverster Wheatsheaf.

Kroll, J. 2008. Creative practice and/as/is/or research: an overview. Conference proceedings for *AAWP 2008: Creativity and Uncertainty* [Website]. Available at: http://aawp.org.au/files/Kroll.pdf. [Accessed June 2009].

Ebert, R., 2003. *Roger Ebert's Movie Yearbook 2004*. Kansas: Andrews McMeel Publishing.

Eco, U., 1986. *Travels in Hyperreality*. New York: Harcourt Brace Jovanovich.

Edelstein, D., 1999. Dark side lite. *Slate*, [Online] 19 May 1999. Available at: http://web.archive.org/web/20000306215502/http://www.slate.com/MovieReview/99-05-19/MovieReview.asp [Accessed 07 Sep 2012].

Eisenberg, A., 2011. Animated or real, both are believable. *The New York Times*, [Online] 27 Aug 2011. Available at: http://www.nytimes.com/2011/08/28/business/technology-blurs-the-line-between-the-animated-and-the-real.html?_r=1 [Accessed 20 Sep 2012].

Eisenstein, S., 1988.*Eisenstein on Disney*, translated by A. Upchurch, edited by J. Leyda. London: Methuen.

—. 1992. A dialectic approach to film form. In: Gerald Mast, et al., eds. *Film Theory and Criticism: Introductory Readings*, 4th edition. New York: Oxford University Press, pp. 138-54.

—. 1998.*The Eisenstein Reader*, translated by R. Taylor & W. Powell, edited by R. Taylor. London: British Film Institute.

Elsaesser, T., 1998. Digital cinema: delivery, event, time. In: Elsaesser, T. & K. Hoffmann eds., *Cinema Futures: Cain, Abel or Cable? The Screen Arts in the Digital Age*, Amsterdam: Amsterdam University Press, pp. 202-22.

Ferguson, H., 2000. *Modernity and Subjectivity: Body, Soul, Spirit*. Charlottesville, London: University Press of Virginia.

Fordham, F., 2007.*Lots of Fun at Finnegans Wake*. Oxford: Oxford University Press.

Fore, S., 2007. Romancing the rotoscope: self-reflexivity and the reality effect in the animations of Jeff Scher. *Animation: an Interdisciplinary Journal,* 2(2): 111-27.

Freud, S., 2009.The uncanny. In: B. Nelson ed., *On Creativity and the Unconscious*. New York: Harper Collins, pp. 122-60.

Gage, J., 1993. *Color and Culture: Practice and Meaning from Antiquity to Abstraction*. Berkeley: University of California Press.

Gallagher, D., 2007. Digital actors in Beowulf are just uncanny. *The New York Times*, [Online] 14 Nov 2007. Available at: http://bits.blogs.nytimes.com/2007/11/14/digital-actors-in-beowulf-are-just-uncanny/ [Accessed 07 Sep 2012].

Gehman C. & S. Reinke eds., 2005.*The Sharpest Point: Animation at the End of Cinema*. Toronto: YYZ Books.

Giannetti, L., 2011. *Understanding Movies*, 12th ed. New York: Pearson Education.

Gilbey, R., 2006. Sun, sea, sand and horror. *New Stateman (UK)*, [Online] 10 Jul 2006. Available at: http://www.newstatesman.com/node/153632 [Accessed 18 Sep 2012].

Ginzburg, C. 2001. *Wooden Eyes: Nine Reflections on Distance*, translated by M. Ryle & K. Soper. New York, Chichester, West Sussex: Columbia University Press.

Graca, M. E., 2006. Cinematic motion by hand. *Animation Studies*, [On line] 1. Available at: http://journal.animationstudies.org/category/volume-1/ [Accessed 19 September 2008]

Greniville, B., 2002. *The Uncanny: Experiments in Cyborg Culture*. London: Arsenal.

Gunning, T., 1990."A frame-up? Or the trick's on us". In: T. Elsaesser & A. Barker eds., *Early Cinema*, London: British Film Institute, pp. 95-103.

—. 2008. Uncanny reflections, modern illusions: sighting the modern optical uncanny. In: J. Collins & J. Jervis eds., *Uncanny Modernity: Cultural Theories, Modern Anxieties*. New York: Palgrave Macmillan.

Han, X., 2009. Interpreting the butterfly dream. *Asian Philosophy,* 19(1).

Harrison, E., 1999. Even an insider found Jar Jar, well, jarring. *Los Angeles Times*, [Online] 21 Jun 1000. Available at: http://articles.latimes.com/1999/jun/21/entertainment/ca-48611 [Accessed 07 Sep 2012].

Harryhausen, R. & T. Dalton, 2008. *A Century of Model Animation: from Melies to Aardman*. London: Aurum Press.

Heath, S., 1978.Notes on suture. *Screen* 18: 48-76.

Hebert, P. 2005. Cinema, animation and the other arts: an unanswered question. In: C. Gehman & S. Reinke eds., *The Sharpest Point: Animation at the End of Cinema*. Toronto: YYZ Books, pp. 179-88.

Heckbert, P., 1986. Survey of texture mapping. *IEEE Computer Graphics and Applications*, [Online] Nov 1986. Available at: http://www.cs.cmu.edu/~ph/texsurv.pdf [Accessed August 2009]

Henricks, R. trans., 1993.*Te-ao Ching*. New York: The Modern Library.

Hernandez, M. L., 2010. Through the looking glass: the self-portrait of the artist and the re-start of animation. *Animation Studies*, 5: 41-50.

Hiltzik, M. & A. Pham, 2001. Synthetic actors guild. *Los Angeles Times*, [Online] 08 May 2001. Available at: http://articles.latimes.com/2001/may/08/news/mn-60707 [Accessed 07 Sep 2012].

Jackman, J. 2007. *Bluescreen Compositing*. Burlington, Oxford: Focal Press.

Jameson, F., 1989.*Postmodernism and Cultural Theories*, translated by X. Tang. Taipei: Hezhi Cultural Publisher.

—.1991.*Postmodernism, or The Cultural Logic of Late Capitalism*. Durham: Duke University Press.

Jervis, J., 2008. Uncanny presence. In: J. Collins & J. Jervis eds., *Uncanny Modernity: Cultural Theories, Modern Anxieties*. New York: Palgrave Macmillan.

Johnson, C., 1999. Ambient Technologies, Uncanny Signs. *Oxford Literary Review*, 21: 117-34.

Markus, H. R. & Kitayama, S., 1991. Culture and the self: implications for cognition, emotion, and motivation. *Psychological Review*, 98: 224-53.

Kelts, R., 2009. Anime is Ill in Japan. *Daily Yomiuri*, June 15, 2009.

Kracauer, S., 1960.*Theory of Film: the Redemption of Physical Reality*. New York: Oxford University Press.

Lasseter, J., 1994. Tickets to animating characters with a computer, notes from course 1 at SIGGRAPH 94.*SIGGRAPH.ORG*, [Online]. Available at:

http://www.siggraph.org/education/materials/HyperGraph/animation/character_animation/principles/lasseter_s94.htm#ask why [Accessed 10 Oct 2012].

Lacan, J., 1977 [1964].*Seminar XI: The Four Fundamental Concepts of Psychoanalysis*, translated by A. Sheridan. London: Penguin.

Lehmann, A., 2009. Invisible work: the representation of artistic practice in digital visual culture. In: A. Bentkowska-Kafel, T. Cashen, H. Gardiner eds., *Digital Visual Culture: Theory and Practice*. Bristol, Chicago: Intellect Books.

Leslie, E., 2004. *Hollywood Flatlands*. London, New York: Verso Books.

Lent, J. A., 2000. Animation in Asia: appropriation, reinterpretation, and adoption or adaptation. *Screening the Past* [website]. Available at: http://www.latrobe.edu.au/screeningthepast/firstrelease/fr1100/jlfr11c.htm [Accessed 11 Oct 2012].

Lister, M. et al., 2003.*New Media: a Critical Introduction*. London and New York: Routledge.

Lowenstein, A., 2007. The Surrealism of the photographic image: Bazin, Barthes, and the digital sweet hereafter. *Cinema Journal*, 46, No. 3, Spring 2007, 54-82.

MacGillivray, C., 2007. How psychophysical perception of motion and image relates to animation practice. Conference paper of *4th International Conference on Computer Graphics, Imaging and Visualization2007*, Bangkok, IEEE Computer Society 2007, [On line]. Available at:
http://csdl2.computer.org/persagen/DLAbsToc.jsp?resourcePath=/dl/proceedings/&toc=comp/proceedings/cgiv/2007/2928/00/2928toc.xml&DOI=10.1109/CGIV.2007.48 . [Accessed 19 Sep 2008]

Manning, E., 2009. *Relationscapes: Movement, Art, Philosophy*. Cambridge, MA, London: MIT Press.

Manovich, L., 2001. *The Language of New Media*. Cambridge, MA, London: MIT Press.

Marx, K., 1990. *Capital: a Critique of Political Economy*, volume 1, translated by B. Fowkes. London: Penguin Books.

McCarthy, E., 2010. Behind the scenes of Splice: interviews with the director and VFX supervisor. *Popular Mechanics*, [Online] 28 Jan 2010. Available at:
http://www.popularmechanics.com/technology/digital/visual-effects/4343953 [Accessed 18 Sep 2012].

McClean, S., 2007.*Digital Storytelling: the Narrative Power of Visual Effects in Film*. Cambridge, Massachusetts: MIT Press. Merleau-Ponty, M., 1964 [1948]. The film and the new psychology. In: *Sense and Non-sense*, translated by H. and P. Dreyfus. Evanston, IL: Northwestern University Press, pp. 48-59.

Merleau-Ponty, M., 1968a [1964].*The Visible and the Invisible*, translated by A. Lingis, edited by C. Lefort. Evanston, IL: Northwestern University Press.

—.1964b [1960].*Signs*, translated by Richard McCleary. Evanston, IL: Northwestern University Press.

—.1970 [1953].*In Praise of Philosophy and Other Essays*, translated by J. O'Neill. Evanston, IL: Northwestern University Press.

Meyer, J.H.F. & R. Land, 2005a. Threshold concepts: an introduction. In J.H.F. Meyer and R. Land eds., *Overcoming barriers to student understanding: threshold concepts and troublesome knowledge.* London: Routledge Falmer, pp.3-18.

Meyer, J.H.F. & R. Land, 2005b. Threshold concepts and troublesome knowledge (2): epistemological considerations and a conceptual framework for teaching and learning. *Higher Education*, Vol. 49, No. 3, 373-388.

Messaris P. & L. Humphreys, 2006. Introduction. In: Messaris, P. & L. Humphreys eds., *Digital Media: Transformations in Human Communication.* New York: Peter Lang Publishing, pp. XV-XIX.

Mike, W. & W. Daniel, 1989. *The Art of Photography: 1839-1989.* New Haven: Yale University Press.

Miller, J., 1978. *Suture (elements of the logic of the signifier)*, translated by J. Rose, *Screen* 18 23-24.

Mitchell, E., 2001. Film review; she's lovely, but alas, she's only software. *New York Times*, [Online] 11 Jul 2001. Available at: http://www.nytimes.com/2001/07/11/movies/film-review-she-s-lovely-but-alas-she-s-only-software.html [Accessed 07 Sep 2012].Mori, M., 1970. The uncanny valley, translated by MacDorman, K. F. & T. Minato.*Energy*, 7(4), pp. 33-35. Available at: http://www.androidscience.com/theuncannyvalley/proceedings2005/uncannyvalley.html. [Accessed 19 September 2008]

Nathan, D., 2010. *The McFarland Baseball Quotations Dictionary.* North Carolina: McFarland & Company.

North, D., 2008. Performing Illusions: Cinema, Special Effects and the Virtual Actor. New York: Columbia University Press.

Oudart, J., 1978. *Cinema and suture*, translated by K. Hanet, *Screen* 18: 35-47.

Perkins, D., 2006. Constructivism and troublesome knowledge. In J. H. F. Meyer and R. Land eds., *Overcoming barriers to student understanding: threshold concepts and troublesome knowledge.* London: Routledge Falmer, pp. 33-47.

Pesimo, R. C., 2007. "Asianizing" animation in Asia: digital content identity construction within the animation landscapes of Japan and Thailand. *Reflections on the Human Condition: Change, Conflict and*

Modernity – The Work of 2004/2005 API Fellows. The Nippon Foundation [pdf], pp. 124-60. Available at: http://www.apimal.org/blogcms/media/13/File/Pesimo.pdf [Accessed 11 Oct 2012].

Pilling, J. 1992. *Women and Animation: A Compendium*. Suffolk: BFI.

Prince, S., 1996. True lies: perceptual realism, digital images, and film theory. *Film Quarterly*, 49(3), pp. 27-37.

—.2004. The emergence of filmic artifacts: cinema and cinematography in the digital era. *Film Quarterly*, 57(3), pp. 24-33.

Ramey, C. H., 2005. The uncanny valley of similarities concerning abortion, baldness, heaps of sand, and humanlike robots. In: *Proceedings of Views of the Uncanny Valley Workshop: IEEE-RAS International Conference on Humanoid Robots*, Tsukuba, Japan, 8-13.

Reinhold, M., 1970.*History of Purple as a Status Symbol in Antiquity*. Brussels: Collection Latomus.

Riggs, Freida, 2007. The infinite quest: Husseri, Bakshi, rotoscope and the ring. In: A. Cholodenko ed., *The Illusion of Life 2: More Essays on Animation*. Sydney: Power Publications.

Robinson, J., 2011. Tintin review: a rip-roaring adventure in The Uncanny Valley.*PAJIBA*, [Online] 22 Dec 2011. Available at: http://www.pajiba.com/film_reviews/tintin-review-a-riproaring-adventure-in-the-uncanny-valley.php [Accessed 20 Sep 2012].

Royle, N., 2003. *The Uncanny*. Manchester: Manchester University Press.

Rose, S., 2011. Tintin and the Uncanny Valley: when CGI gets too real. *The Guardian*, [Online] 27 Oct 2011. Available at: http://www.guardian.co.uk/film/2011/oct/27/tintin-uncanny-valley-computer-graphics [Accessed 08 Sep 2012].

Sartre, J., 2004. *The Imaginary: A Phenomenological Psychology of the Imagination* (Revised Edition), revised by A. Elkaim-Sartre, translated by J. Webber. London, New York: Routledge.

Schwarzbaum, L., 2010. Movie Review: Splice. *Entertainment Weekly*, [Online] 04 Jun 2010. Available at: http://www.ew.com/ew/article/0,,20388505,00.html [Accessed 18 Sep 2010].

Scott, A. O., 2005. The unreal road from Toontown to "Sin City". The New York Times, [Online] 24 Apr 2005. Available at: http://www.nytimes.com/2005/04/24/movies/24scot.html?ex=1271995200&en=83f36c443f1c41eb&ei=5088&partner=rssnyt&emc=rss&_r=0 [Accessed 11 Oct 2012].

Shklovshy, V., 1917.Art as technique. In L.T. Lemon & M. Reis.eds., 1965, *Russian Formalist Criticism*. Nebraska: University of Nebraska Press, pp. 3-24.

Silverman, K., 1983. *The Subject of Semiotics*. New York: Oxford

University Press.

Small, E. S. & E. Levinson, 1989.Toward a theory of animation.*Velvet Light Trap,* 24: 67-74.

Solomon, C. ed., 1987.*The Art of the Animated Image: an anthology*. Los Angeles: The American Film Institute.

Solomon, C., 1989. *Enchanted Drawings: The History of Animation*. New York: Alfred A. Knopf.

Staples, B., 1999.Editorial observer; shuffling through star war.*The New York Times*, [Online] 20 Jun 1999. Available at: http://www.nytimes.com/1999/06/20/opinion/editorial-observer-shuffling-through-the-star-wars.html [Accessed 07 Sep 2012].

Sullivan, G. 2005. *Art Practice as Research*. California, London, New Delhi: Sage Publications.

Surman, D., 2003/2004. CGI animation: pseudorealism, perception and possible worlds. *Gamasutra Education*, [On line]. Available at: http://www.gamasutra.com/education/theses/20040928/DavidSurmanThesis.pdf. [Accessed 8 July 2008]

Taiwan's Council of Labor Affairs, 2012. *Survey on Wage by Occupation* (職類別薪資調查報告). Taipei: Council of Labor Affairs.

Taylor, A. 2005. Research as a dialectical activity: writing a long poem in Rome, *Speculation and Innovation: Applying Practice Led Research in the Creative Industries. Queensland University of Technology*, [Website]. Available at: http://www.speculation2005.net [Accessed June 2010].

Telotte, J. P., 2010. *Animating Space: From Mickey to WALL-E. Lexington*. Kentucky: The University Press of Kentucky.

Tezuka, O., 1989. *Osamu Tezuka Story: I am Son-Goku*, directed by M. Hata, Rintaro. Tezuka production Company [TV movie].

Thomas, F. & O. Johnston, 1981. *The Illusion of Life: Disney Animation*. New York: Walt Disney Productions.

Thompson, K., 1980. Implications of the cel animation technique. In: T. Lauretis& S. Heath eds., 1980. *The Cinematic Apparatus*. New York: St. Martin's, pp. 106-20.

—.1981. *Eisenstein's* Ivan the Terrible: *A Neo-Formalist Analysis*. Princeton, NJ: Princeton University Press.

—.1988. *Breaking the Glass Armor: Neoformalist Film Analysis*. Princeton, NJ: Princeton University Press.

—.2009. Formalism. In: P. Livingston & C. Plantingam, eds., *The Routledge Companion to Philosophy and Film*. London, New York: Routledge.

Tie, W., 2004. The psychic life of governmentality. *Culture, Theory and Critique*, 45(2): 161-76.

Trahair, L., 1991. For the noise of a fly. In: A. Cholodenko ed., *The*

Illusion of Life: Essays on Animation. Sydney: Power Publication.
Virilio, P., 1991. *The Lost Dimension*. New York: Semiotest(e).
Ward, P., 2004. Rotoshop in context: computer rotoscoping and animation aesthetics. *Animation Journal*, 12, 2004: 32-52.
Weight, J., 2006. I, apparatus, you: a technosocial introduction to creative practice. *Convergence: The International Journal of Research into New Media Technologies*, 12(4): 413-46.
Wells, P., 1998. *Understanding Animation*. London & New York: Routledge.
—.2002. *Animation and America*. New Brunswick, New Jersey: Rutgers University Press.
—.2006. *The Fundamentals of Animation*. Switzerland: AVA Publishing SA.
—.2009. *The Animated Bestiary: Animals, Cartoons, and Culture*. New Brunswick, New Jersey: Rutgers University Press.
Wells, P. & J. Hardstaff, 2008. *Re-imaging Animation: The Changing Face of the Moving Image*. Lausanne, Switzerland: AVA Publishing.
Whitaker, H. & J. Halas, 1981. *Timing for Animation*. Oxford, Burlington: Focal Press.
Williams, R. 2001.*The Animator's Survival Kit*. London, New York: Faber and Faber.
—.2004. *Art Theory: an Historical Introduction*. Oxford: Blackwell Publishing.
Wolchover, N., 2011. What scientists are doing about creepy CGI humans.*NBCNEWS.COM*, [Online] 18 Oct 2011. Available at: http://www.msnbc.msn.com/id/44953405/ns/technology_and_science-science/t/what-scientists-are-doing-about-creepy-cgi-humans/#.UEnYPLLN-ae [Accessed 07 Sep 2012].
Zhu, Y. & S. Rosen, 2010. *Art, Politics and Commerce in Chinese Cinema*. Hong Kong: Hong Kong University Press.

Films

300, 2007. [Film] Directed by Zack Snyder. California: Legendary Pictures; Arizona: Virtual Studios; California: Cruel and Unusual Films; Tennessee: Atmosphere Pictures; California: Hollywood Gang.
Alice in Wonderland, 2010.[Film].Directed by Tim Burton. California: Roth Films; California: Team Todd; California: Tim Burton Productions. California: The Zanuck Company.
Alice's Mysterious Mystery, 1924. [Film] Directed by Walt Disney & UbIwerks.
Angry Kid series, 1999 - present. [TV programme]. Directed by Darren

Walsh. Bristol (UK): Aardman Animations.
Animated Self-Portraits, 1989. [Video] Complied by David Ehrlich consisting of 27 animators.
Animator vs. Animation, 2006. [Film] Directed by Alan Becker.
Beowulf, 2007. [Film] Directed by Robert Zemeckis.
Betty Boop's Bamboo Isle, 1932. [Film] Directed by Dave Fleisher & Shamus Culhane. California: Paramount Pictures.
Cendrillon, 1899. [Film] Directed by George Melies.
Christmas Carol, 2009. [Film] Directed by Robert Zemeckis.
City Paradise, 2004. [Video] Directed by Gaelle Denis.
Cows & Cows & Cows, 2010. [Video] Directed by Cyriak.
Da NaoHua Shi, 1927. [Film] Directed by Wan Brothers.
Doll Face, 2005. [Video] Directed by Andy Huang.
Everything Will be OK, 2006. [Film] Directed by Don Hertzfeldt.
Fantasmagorie, 1908. [Film] Directed by Emile Cohl.
Final Fantasy: The Spirits Within, 2001. Directed by Hironobu Sakaguchi. Hawaii: Square Pictures.
Fun and Fancy Free, 1947. [Film] California: Walt Disney Productions.
Godzilla, 1954. [Film] Directed by Ishirō Honda. Tokyo: Toho.
Harpa, 1979. [Film] Directed by Raoul Servais,
Hulk, 2003. [Film] Directed by Ang Lee.
Humorous Phases of Funny Faces, 1906. [Film] Directed by J. Stuart Blackton.
King Kong, 1933. [Film] Directed by Merian C. Cooper & Ernest B. Schoedsack. New York: RKO Radio Pictures.
King Kong, 2005. [Film] Directed by Peter Jackson. California: Universal Studios.
I move, so I am, 1998. [Video] Directed by Gerrit Van Dijk.
La cavernemaudite, 1898. [Film] Directed by George Melies.
La Colonne de Feu, 1899. [Film] Directed by George Melies.
La Sexilinea, 1977. [Video] Directed by Osvaldo Cavandoli.
Le Royaume De Fées, 1903. [Film] Directed by George Melies.
Lighting Sketches, 1907. [Film] Directed by J. Stuart Blackton.
Madame Tutli-putli, 2008. [Video] Directed by Chris Lavis & Maciek Szczerbowski. Montreal (Canada): National Film Board of Canada.
Manipulation, 1991. [Video] Directed by Daniel Greaves.
Mighty Joe Young, 1949. [Film] Directed by Ernest B. Schoedsack. New York: RKO Radio Pictures.
Mighty Joe Young, 1998. [Film] Directed by Ron Underwood. New York: RKO Radio Pictures.
Momotaro's Divine Sea Warrior, 1945. Directed by Mitsuyo Seo.
Monster House, 2006. [Film] Directed by Gil Kenan. California: Relativity Media; California: Image Movers; California: Amblin Entertainment.

Neighbours, 1953. [Film] Directed by Norman McLaren
Nippy's Nightmare, 1911. [Film] Directed by Willis O'Brian.
Out of the Inkwell: Tantalizing Fly, 1920. [Film] Directed by Max Fleisher. California: Paramount Pictures.
Picnic with Weissmann, 1968. [Film] Directed by Svankmajer.
Pirate of the Caribbean: Dead Man's Chest, 2006. [Film] Directed by Gore Verbinski. California: Jerry Bruckheimer Films.
Pretty, Dead, 2010. [Video] Directed by Jeff Scher.
Princess Iron Fan, 1941. [Film] Directed by the Wan brothers.
Princess Nicotine, 1909. [Film] Directed by J. Stuart Blackton.
Repo Men, 2010.Directed by Miguel Sapochnik. California: Relativity Media; California: Stuber Pictures.
Rise of the Planet of the Apes, 2011. [Film] Directed by Rupert Wyatt. California: 20th Century Fox; California: Dune Entertainment; California: Chernin Entertainmment.
Snow White and the Seven Dwarfs, 1937. [Film] California: Walt Disney Productions.
Song of the South, 1946. [Film] California: Walt Disney Productions.
Star Wars Episode I: Phantom Menace, 1999. [Film] Directed by George Lucas. California: Lucasfilm.
Sin City, 2005. [Film] Directed by Frank Miller. Texas: Troublemaker Studios.
Slice, 2009. [Film] Directed by Vincenzo Natali. California: Dark Castle Entertainment; Toronto (Canada): Copper Heart Entertainment; Neuilly-sur-Seine (France): Gaumont.
Sky Captain and the World of Tomorrow, 2004. [Film] Directed by Kerry Conran. Rome (Italy): Filmauro; New York: Brooklyn Films.
Speed Racer, 2008. [Film] Directed by Wachowski Brothers. Victoria (Australia): Village Roadshow Pictures; California: Silver Pictures; Illinois: Anarchos Productions; London: Velocity Productions; Potdam (Germany): Sechste Babelsberg Film.
Surf Up, 2007. [Film] Directed by Ash Brannon & Chris Buck. California: Sony Pictures Animation; California: Sony Pictures Imageworks.
The Adventures of Tintin: Secret of the Unicorn, 2011. [Film] Directed by Steven Spielberg. California: Nickelodeon Movies; California: Amblin Entertainment; California: The Kennedy' Marshall Company; Wellington (New Zealand): Wing Nut Films.
The Arrival of a Train at La Ciotat Station, 1895. [Film] Directed by Lumière Brothers.
The Cameraman's Revenge, 1912. [Film] Directed by Ladislas Starevich.
The Enchanted Drawing, 1900. [Film] Directed by J. Stuart Blackton.
The Execution of Mary Queen of Scot, 1895. [Film] Directed by Alfred Clark.

Fallen Art, 2004. [Video] Directed by Tomasz Bagiński.
The Haunted Hotel, 1907. [Film] Directed by J. Stuart Blackton.
The Fuccons: The Whole Fuccon Show, 2008. [DVD]. Directed by Yoshimasa Ishibashi. Released by ADV.
The Incredible Hulk, 2008. [Film] Directed by Louis Leterrier.
The Lord of the Rings film trilogy, 2001-2003. [Film] Directed by Peter Jackson. Wellington (New Zealand): Wing Nut Films; New Jersey: Saul Zaentz.
The Lost World, 1925. [Film] Directed by Harry O. Hoyt.
The Lunch Hound, 1927. [Film] Directed by Lantz Walter.
The Melomaniac (1903). [Film] Directed by George Melies.
The Mummy, 1999. [Film] Directed by Stephen Sommers.California: Universal Studios.
The Polar Express, 2004. [Film] Directed by Robert Zemeckis.
The Secret Adventures of Tom Thumb, 1993. [Film] Directed by Bolex Brothers.
The Three Caballeros, 1945. [Film] California: Walt Disney Productions.
The Triangle (1982). [Film] Directed by PriitParn.
The Wizard of Speed and Time, 1979. [Video] Directed by Mike Jittlov.
Un Homme de tete, 1898. [Film] Directed by George Melies.
Vicious Cycles, 1967. [Film] Directed by Chuck Menville& Len Janson,
WALL-E, 2009. [Film] Directed by Andrwe Stanton. California: Pixar.
Western Spaghetti, 2008. [Video] Directed by PES.
Winsor McCay, the Famous Cartoonist of the N.Y. Herald and His Moving Comics (or Gertie the Dinosaur), 1914. [Film] Directed by Winsor McCay.
You ought to be in Pictures, 1940. [Film] Warner Brothers.